ARTHUR GUITERMAN

BRAVE LAUGHTER

by

Arthur Guiterman

WITH AN INTRODUCTION BY

Eleanor Graham

Frontispiece

BOOKS INC., DISTRIBUTED BY

E. P. Dutton & Company, Inc.

NEW YORK

1943

FIRST PRINTING . . . SEPTEMBER 1943
SECOND PRINTING . . NOVEMBER 1943

S. A. JACOBS, THE GOLDEN EAGLE PRESS
MOUNT VERNON, N. Y.

DEDICATION

Dear Friends

When I am gone, if it should give you pleasure,
Say what you will of me in prose or measure;
But should you chance to feel the other way
About my "life or letters," leave 'em lay.
Whatever you may purpose I allow,
God bless you, for you'll do it anyhow.

CONTENTS

	PAGE
Dedication	5
Acknowledgment	11
Arthur Guiterman by HAROLD TROWBRIDGE PULSIFER	13
Introduction by ELEANOR GRAHAM	17
WHERE THE ROAD MIGHT LEAD	75
Utility	77
Courage and Mirth	78
The Forerunners	79
Parable for Conquerors	80
The Victor	81
The Little Bewildered People	82
Pilot	83
The Veterans	84
Crossroads	85
Epitaph	85
The Eternal Question	86
Sanctuary	87
The Child	88
Old Wives' Tale	89
Be a Good Sport	90
Inventors	91
Heredity	92
Appeaser's Hymn	93
The Pitcher that Went to the Well	94
The Law	96
To Commodore Matthew Calbraith Perry	97
The Eagle	97
A Scrap of Paper	98
A White Paper	98

CONTENTS

	PAGE
The Freedom of the Seize	99
Fashions for Fascists	101
Diplomatic Correspondence	102
"Let Us Now Praise Famous Men"	103
The Miracle of Robert de Baudricourt	104
Honor	107
Scene in Hell	107
Neutrality	108
To C. I. O. and A. F. L.	109
U. S. A.	109
"We've Got It to Do"	110
Green Mountain Graveyard	112
Iron Master	113
The Rocking Chair	116
The Answer	119
Among the Angels	119
Vermont Marble	120
Planting an English Oak	121
Brave Laughter	122
HOMO SAP	123
Brief Essay on Man	125
Outline of Evolution	126
Our Absurd Past	128
The Chip on the Shoulder	129
Note for Legislators	130
The Ides	130
Fortune Telling	131
What Are the Short Waves Saying	133
Real-Estate Business	134
Names and Numbers	137
Farewell to the Aquarium	139
At La Guardia Field	141
A Fable for Litigants	142

8

CONTENTS

	PAGE
Wedding Gift Alphabet	143
Aquarium Note	147
Sunday School Story	148
Motto for a Beauty Parlor	149
Excelsior	149
Grandeur	150
You and Your Conscience	152
Everything in Its Place	153
The Paradise of Children	154
Sincere Sympathy	155
Retribution	156
Subject to Change without Notice	157
Reprieved	158
The Army Mule	159
Outdoor Furniture	161
Contentment	162
Suggesting a Compromise	163
Weather Report	164
The Imp of Forgetfulness	165
The King's English	166
Poem for Purists	168
Victorian Relapse	170
What Every Publisher Knows	171
ADAM TO EVE	173
Adam to Eve	175
Serenade	176
The Trail	177
The Cabin	178
Lightness	180
Relic	181
Are You a Man or a Mouse?	182
Compensation	184

CONTENTS

	PAGE
Morning Song	184
The Steel Wedding	185
Treasure-Trove	187
The Unseen Lover	188
So Little	190
Lost, Strayed, or Stolen	191
Flamingo Dance	193
Meteor	194
CLEAN WATERS	195
Clean Waters	197
Dream Trout	198
Hillborn	199
Country Doctor	201
News from Vermont	203
The State Seal Pine	206
To a Cicada	208
Bullied by Birds	209
Against Gardeners	210
Wild Orchard	212
First Snowfall	212
Compliments of the Seasons	213
Short Cut	214
Elfin Economy	215
Malt and Hops	217
Sea Birds	218
For All Young Things	218
Epitaph on a Gallant Mare	219
The Desolater	220
Storm	221
Going and Staying	222
Harvest Home	223
Winterproof	224

ACKNOWLEDGMENT

THE compilers of this collection thank the editors of *The New York Herald Tribune*, *The New York Times*, *The Saturday Evening Post*, *The New Yorker*, *House and Garden*, *The New York Sun*, *Good Housekeeping*, *The Saturday Review of Literature*, *Forum*, *This Week* and many other magazines and newspapers for permission to reprint poems that originally appeared in their pages.

ARTHUR GUITERMAN

"Good-by," he said, "until the spring!"—
And though no spring will find him here,
Forever now his name will bring
Green leaves, bright blossoms, shining clear.

Loving the touch of heart and mind
As deeply as his distant hills,
With every instinct to be kind,
He did not shrink from warring wills.

The pen that brought the living joy
Quick dancing in a host of eyes
Had peerless power to destroy
The poison of a thousand lies.

Dearer than friends — than length of days
He held the honor of his land.
If you would crown his life with bays,
Guard all he loved, with heart and hand!

HAROLD TROWBRIDGE PULSIFER

INTRODUCTION

INTRODUCTION

BECAUSE it is good to hear him speaking in his own words, this Introduction begins with a quotation from one of Arthur Guiterman's letters, written in 1936:

"Neither of us believes in glossing over the fact that there is overmuch evil and suffering in the world, but we know that this is something more than a vale of tears, and that concentrating on gloom is morbid and unwholesome and does no good. . . . As nearly as I have a general philosophy, I tried to express it in the envoy of my poem, 'The Eagle.' [1] My feeling is that Man must work out his own salvation, and that though progress or evolution seems to us painfully slow, it goes ahead with increasing speed 'through battles lost and won.' I can't see how anyone who knows history at all can deny our real gains. Of course we must fight against evil; but there is such a thing as fighting joyously and hopefully. I've known joyous fighters, and found them much more valuable than gloomy, fanatical revolutionaries, full of hates and pessimisms. And in the meantime, I do believe that we should add to the common stock of human happiness, by no means neglecting our own. I saw recently a quotation from some modern philosopher, I think maybe Henri Bergson, to the effect that 'The

[1] *Death and General Putnam and 101 Other Poems*, E. P. Dutton & Co. (New York, 1935), p. 78.

17

universe is a machine for the manufacture of gods.' If so, let's try to help make them gods of courage and gladness. Literary crape-hangers must hang crape, I presume, but that isn't your natural vocation, so why bother about it, just because perverted pundits think that Gloom is the only High Art? Also, I know that it is natural and necessary that some should be concentrating on new or improved social orders; but a world without 'moonlight and blossoms and gentleness and love' would not be a good world to live in under any social order. People are very fond of demanding that you should not be afraid to say what *they* think; well, don't be afraid to tell them and the world what *you* think."

Arthur Guiterman used to say laughingly that there was nothing in the circumstances of his birth to prevent his becoming President of the United States any time he had a mind to. For though he was born in Vienna on November 20, 1871, and his father, Alexander Guiterman had been born in the Kingdom of Bavaria, Alexander had come to America as a young lad and had been a citizen of this country for years before he married Louisa Wolf of Cincinnati. The couple had gone to Vienna soon after their marriage. There three of their children, Edward, Helène, and Arthur, came into the world — all registered immediately at the American Legation as natural-born Americans. Louisa Wolf Guiterman was of pioneer stock. Since two of his great-grandfathers were buried in the valley of the Ohio, it does not seem strange that although chance decreed that Arthur be born abroad, he was to be called by Joyce Kilmer "the most American of poets."

Arthur was not yet three when the family returned to New York — so that his "recollections" of Vienna were only the stories he had heard his mother repeat — that his first baby-talk was in German rather than in English, and that his nurse had taught him to recognize and identify the emperors, kings, and queens who often passed through the streets of the Austrian capital in solemn procession.

His real memories were of New York, where, with the exception of a couple of years, he spent all of his boyhood. Like other children, he played baseball and shinny and built bonfires for roasting potatoes. He was an active child, but undersized; and his wise mother encouraged him to skate and to take part in sports. He loved animals, and his earliest ambition was to become a naturalist. That may be why *Hiawatha* was the first poem to make a deep impression on him.

The family went for long summer vacations in the White Mountains, and there Arthur found a love for hills and the outdoors that he cherished all his life. At the time of their first trip, when he was seven and a half, they arrived at Jefferson, New Hampshire, at dusk. As they rode from the station to the hotel, the quiet summer evening was agleam with fireflies. To the little city boy who had never before been up late enough to see them,

they were pure magic, and he was so impressed that he
wrote his first poem:

> In the summer evening
> Over the hill and dale
> Fireflies are twinkling,
> Making little dashes,
> While the light it flashes
> By the little brook.
> Fireflies prancing,
> The light goes dancing
> Through the bushes by the lone pathway on the hill,
> And the lights are dancing,
> Dancing while we are asleep and still.

There could be no better picture of the little fellow at
that time than he himself drew in 1924 in his "Blessing
on Little Boys": [2]

> God, bless all little boys who look like Puck,
>   With wide eyes, wider mouths and stick-out ears,
> Rash little boys who stay alive by luck
>   And Heaven's favor in this world of tears,
> Ten-thousand-question-asking little boys,
>   Rapid of hand and foot and thought as well,
> Playing with gorgeous fancies more than toys,
>   Heroes of what they dream, but never tell;
> Father, in your vast playground let them know
>   The loveliness of ocean, star and hill;
> Protect from every bitterness and woe
>   Your heedless little acolytes, and still
> Grant me the grace, I beg upon my knees,
> Not to forget that I was one of these.

[2] *Saturday Evening Post*, March 15, 1924 and *Death and General
Putnam and 101 Other Poems*, p. 50.

About 1879, his father's business as an owner of the Fairfield Chemical Works took the family to Bridgeport, Connecticut, where to the children P. T. Barnum was the important man. Every spring, Barnum celebrated his birthday by inviting all the local youngsters to the circus. Years later, Arthur paid tribute to the benign old gentleman as "King of the Realm of Let's Pretend." [3]

After their return to New York when Arthur was ten, his sister Eleanor was born. They were a large household in the high-stooped brownstone on West Fifty-eighth Street; for Louisa's mother, with her son, her daughter, and her granddaughter, now lived with them.

Arthur's mother, Louisa, was the dominant figure of the family, though always quietly dominant. Gifted with quick humor, unusual insight into character, and a keen sense of justice, she also developed a tact that made her the constant mediator and adjuster of difficulties among the assorted individualists living under one roof. She was a brilliant pianist and was always willing to play for the children who gathered around to sing not only the current tunes but the old Civil War songs she had brought from her girlhood in Cincinnati.

Arthur went to Public School 69 at near-by Fifty-fourth Street. Playing with other boys in vacant lots, he began to overcome the frailness which had been

[3] "An American Immortal," *Lyric Laughter*, E. P. Dutton & Co. (New York, 1939), p. 13.

noticeable when he was very young. The red setter, Bute, who shared the top floor front room with the boys, was his constant companion. The dog was supposed to sleep on the "Spartan Couch," an old sofa with a door nailed across the seat, camouflaged by an afghan which concealed its brutal hardness. But the setter pup knew comfort; and though he started the night on the sofa, in the morning he would always be found settled in the small of Arthur's back, occupying the middle of the bed, while Arthur clung to the very edge. Bute is mentioned affectionately in the poem, "Little Lost Pup." [4]

The children all read a great deal. The house was full of books, and they were never told what to read or what not to read. Arthur loved Cooper's Indian stories. He reveled in Scott and Shakespeare and preferred Thackeray to Dickens. Bound volumes of *The Youth's Companion* and *St. Nicholas* were annual Christmas gifts to which all the children looked forward.

In those days there was no high school, so when he was graduated from grammar school, he spent five years at the College of the City of New York. An uneven student, poor in mathematics and good in English and history, he was chiefly interested in dramatics and athletics. He rode a high wheel; took part in lacrosse, hockey, and rowing; played tennis; and went out for track, where he was an excellent sprinter. Being physically well co-ordinated by nature, he shone in any sport

---

[4] *Death and General Putnam and 101 Other Poems*, p. 114.

in which a light frame and great agility were advantageous. Although he was also class poet and secretary, he still had time for college theatricals. Of course, there were no girls in the dramatic club, and his slender build fitted him for playing the heroine, opposite his good friend, James K. Hackett, who was to become the country's matinée idol. When Hackett made his great success as Macbeth in London, he wrote to Arthur: "But I only wish Mrs. Pat Campbell had been as good a leading lady as you used to be."

Writing of his college days some forty years after, for the newspaper of the City College of New York Arthur said,[5] "What I think was good for all of us was that we put things through ourselves, without direction and without assistance. We had no gymnasium, we had no theatre, we had no athletic field, we had no endowments. By its annual performance, the dramatic club paid its own expenses and earned a few hundred dollars which helped to finance all branches of athletics. Not that the faculty was altogether unsympathetic, but in everything we depended upon the initiative, enterprise and energy of the student body."

In spite of his many activities, he read as much as ever, and added Tennyson, Byron, Macaulay, and Holmes to his list of favorites. He had always loved old ballads, and his interest in Macaulay probably helped to shape his own style. He admired Byron as a technician as well

[5] *The Campus*, November 16, 1931.

as a poet, and was fond of pointing out his clever rhymes. In 1923, when a newspaper syndicate asked him to name the ten books he had enjoyed most, he compiled the following list:

Quentin Durward
Pendennis
Knickerbocker's History of New York
Shakespeare's *As You Like It, Macbeth, Hamlet,* and *Henry IV*
Byron's poems
Through the Looking Glass
Thomas Bailey Aldrich's *The Story of a Bad Boy*
Rossiter Johnson's *Phaeton Rogers*
Kim
Huckleberry Finn

Besides their beloved Hackett, the class of '91 had many members who later achieved fame. Among them were Rubin Goldmark, composer; Joseph Hertz, Chief Rabbi of the British Empire; Louis Van Norman, journalist and member of the diplomatic service; Emanuel Libman, diagnostician; A. A. Berg, surgeon and authority on rare books; and Sol Stroock, philanthropist and administrator of charities.

Graduated from college with the Ward medal for English composition, Arthur went out in the midst of a depression to find a job. He was immature in appearance: about five feet seven, slender and wiry, with grey-blue eyes and curly reddish-brown hair. His athletics and outdoor life gave him a ruddy complexion, and there was about him a certain Puckish quality that was always to make him seem younger than he was. At that time, he looked more like sixteen than his actual twenty years. He refused to wear the hard derby hat of the period; and while he preferred going bareheaded, at a pinch he tolerated a soft fedora.

The first work he did was on a trade paper, *The Jewelers' Weekly*, and his salary was five dollars a week. His initial assignment was to compile a directory, and a monotonous job it must have been; but it led to the editorship of two trade papers. It also gave him a useful knowledge of the mechanics of publishing. In 1935, when Arthur was exchanging reminiscences with Irving Bacheller and Joseph C. Lincoln, they discovered that all three of them had served their literary apprenticeship on trade papers.

New York was very dear to him, and he had delved deep into the tales and legends of Manhattan's early days. His ballads about the island began to appear in the newspapers and magazines. Another abiding interest of his was the study of the wisdom of the East, and through the years he published hundreds of proverbs in clear, scintillating couplets or quatrains. Many came out in *The Youth's Companion*. It gave him particular pleasure to be published in that magazine and in *St. Nicholas* because of his boyhood devotion to them. Though he was to add much to the world's laughter, his early interest in Oriental philosophy may be responsible for the development of the deep-hearted, intensely serious humanism which underlay all his sparkle and fun.

It was soon after college that he discovered Kipling's early stories in the newspapers, and appreciated them so much that he clipped them and pasted them in a scrap-book. He especially liked "Soldiers Three," and said of its author, "We're going to hear more from this man."

In 1898 when the Spanish-American War was threatening, Arthur wrote a stirring ballad entitled "The Call to the Colors." [6] That and "The Rush of the Oregon" [7] which followed a month later have been considered among the best poems that came out of the war. Not content to express his patriotism in ink, the young poet had tried to get into the Navy, but was rejected on account of his eyesight. He continued to write mainly on patriotic and nature themes. As his name became known, the periodicals that had previously accepted his contributions gratis, began to pay for them. Fans watched the "southeast corner" of the *Times*' editorial page for his poems which appeared with increasing frequency.

Arthur was always interested in politics. When the Good Government Clubs were formed in 1892, he belonged to Club C, and worked with tongue and pen against boss rule. Then, his particular idol became Theodore Roosevelt, the energetic young aristocrat who

[6] *New York Mail and Express*, April 11, 1898 and *A Ballad-Maker's Pack*, Harper and Brothers (New York, 1921), p. 175.

[7] *New York Times*, May 8, 1898 and *A Ballad-Maker's Pack*, p. 179.

had rolled up his sleeves and entered public life with a zest that was making people gasp. In the course of his career, Arthur celebrated T. R. often in verse, first indirectly with the poem called "The Rough Riders." [8] Among the other tributes were "An American," [9] "Roosevelt Men," [10] "His Future," [11] and the spirited "Our Colonel" [12] which appeared a few days after Roosevelt's death:

> Deep loving, well knowing
> His world and its blindness,
> A heart overflowing
> With measureless kindness,
>
> Undaunted in labor,
> And Death was a trifle;
> Steel-true as a saber,
> Direct as a rifle,
>
> All Man in his doing,
> All Boy in his laughter,
> He fronted, unruing,
> The Now and Hereafter,

[8] *The Criterion*, December 1898 and *A Ballad-Maker's Pack*, p. 182.

[9] *Leslie's Weekly*, July 7, 1904.

[10] *Song and Laughter*, E. P. Dutton & Co. (New York, 1929), p. 200.

[11] *Collier's*, March 6, 1909.

[12] *New York Tribune*, January 14, 1919 and *Death and General Putnam and 101 Other Poems*, p. 69.

A storm-battling cedar,
  A comrade, a brother;
Oh, such was our leader,
  Beloved as no other.

When weaker souls faltered
  His courage remade us
Whose tongue never paltered,
  Who never betrayed us.

His hand on your shoulder
  All honors exceeding,
What breast but was bolder
  Because he was leading!

And still in our trouble,
  In peace or in war-time,
His word shall redouble
  Our strength as aforetime.

When wrongs cry for righting
  No odds shall appall us;
To clean, honest fighting
  Again he will call us,

And, cowboys or doughboys,
  We'll follow his drum, boys,
Who never said, "Go, boys!"
  But always said, "Come, boys!"

The poet loved and honored Roosevelt throughout his
life, ranking him with Washington and Lincoln. Although they met only a couple of times, there was no

person who had a greater influence on Arthur's thought and character.

His social life during his young manhood was altogether informal. His companions were of the outdoor sort who met often to take long walks or bicycle rides in groups. His best friend was Albert Heymann, a steady, dependable chap whose scrubbed, rosy appearance was characteristic of his Dutch ancestry, his neatness an amusing contrast to Arthur's carelessness. Albert once said that Arthur had two costumes — a bicycle suit and a dinner coat, and you never could tell which one he would wear. The young men did much of their calling on girls together, belonged to "sociables" and Shakespeare clubs. In winter, they all skated on the lake in Central Park or went up to Woodlands or Van Cortlandt on a Sunday, taking lunches with them. Arthur's beautiful older sister, Helène, married; and his little sister, Eleanor, had grown up to be a beloved companion. He encouraged her in her literary efforts at Normal College, saw that she went out for basketball, and taught her to play a snappy game of tennis. Until his mother died in 1902, he was so comfortable at home that perhaps he was not ambitious enough to struggle to establish himself as a writer. His father was a quiet retiring man and not the type to encourage confidences from the children.

By now, Arthur had graduated from the most tedious kind of hack work, such as compiling trade directories;

but at no time did he consider any honest writing beneath his dignity. He wrote poems to pictures so successfully that people commented on how well the artist had caught *his* idea. Hovering around the magazines, he made himself generally useful. He was known and liked by the staff of the *Woman's Home Companion*, and frequently took the place of a department head who was ill or on vacation, sometimes editing "Sam Loyd's Puzzle Page" or the section "About People," and even occasionally writing under the signature of "Aunt Janet" as editor of children's contributions. Later he did the same kind of work for *The Literary Digest*, substituting at various times for the editors of *Religious News* and *Scientific News*. He liked editorial work, and it did not strangle his muse. In 1905, his verses appeared in print forty-eight times in contrast to five times in 1898.

After Louisa's death, the reduced household dispersed. Eleanor, graduated from college, kept house for her father and brother. Arthur was now able to devote more of his time to the kind of writing he always wanted to do. Though he tried his hand at stories, playlets, and articles, poetry was definitely his medium. He told a friend, "I can write as good prose as the next man, but I can write better poetry."

In July, 1906, the *Woman's Home Companion* published "Strictly Germ-Proof." Arthur often prefaced the reading of those verses about "the Antiseptic Baby and

the Prophylactic Pup" by saying that they were written
in the early days of antisepsis, when people "boiled
everything but the baby." The *Companion* received the
poem enthusiastically, and so did everyone who read it.
In fact, it proved so popular that half a dozen people
claimed its authorship, and for several years Arthur was
kept busy proving that "Strictly Germ-Proof" was his
poem and no one else's.

The story of Arthur Guiterman's courtship is as
romantic as one could wish. In 1906, he met Vida Lindo
at a dance and was immediately attracted by her viva-
cious, nineteen-year-old loveliness. That April, Vida
was in the midst of rehearsals for an amateur performance of Jerome K. Jerome's *Sunset*. She asked her new
acquaintance if he would take part in the play, and was
delighted to find that he was an excellent actor. Soon
after the presentation of the play, they were secretly
engaged — secretly because Arthur was not yet finan-
cially able to undertake the responsibilities of marriage,
and Vida was willing to wait. But her father, Joshua
Lindo, full of paternal pride in his youngest daughter,
finally heard of the engagement and demanded that it be
broken. He had met Arthur only a few times, but he
refused to think of him as a suitor for his daughter's
hand. He was "only a poet!" Mr. Lindo probably im-
agined his daughter living in a garret and sharing a poet's
crust, and he turned from that prospect indignantly.

Even if Arthur did come of a good substantial family, the fact remained that he was a poet. When Vida argued that she was not expecting an immediate marriage but was willing to wait until her writer could prove himself, that was not enough. The proud paterfamilias, born in Venezuela where men ruled their households like emperors, demanded a promise that she would not see Arthur again. But Vida was her father's own daughter in determination, and would make no such pledge.

Joshua Lindo had gone to Panama as a young man, and since many of his family still lived there, he decided to send Vida to visit Panama relatives for a year. Surely that would cure her of her madness! The twenty-year-old girl readily agreed to the trip, for it seemed to offer at least a respite from the unhappy situation at home. She and Arthur knew they could not begin housekeeping on the little that Arthur was making; and if they kept on seeing each other, life at home would be too unpleasant. Time was what the lovers needed.

Later when she spoke of those days, Vida would say, "I was sent to Panama for a year to forget Arthur. I stayed a year and a half, and remembered him!"

Arthur, too, remembered. Vida returned to New York on February 23, 1909, and on March 11, they were married. It was not that Mr. Lindo relented. By this time his opposition had become a fixed idea, and when he heard that his daughter had met her suitor at a masked ball, he demanded dramatically that she "choose between them." There was only one choice possible.

Although Arthur had been writing for a long time, his work had been desultory, and there had been no sudden blossoming into early fame. But while Vida was "doing time," as she called it, in Panama, the first slim volume from his pen appeared, brought out in 1907 by Paul Elder. It was called *Betel Nuts*, and it was a collection of proverbs which were "ever in the mouths of the people of Hindustan, giving spice and color to their speech even as the Betel Nut — the chewing gum of the Orient — spices the breath and reddens the lips of the folk of the bazaars."[13] The pithy couplets and quatrains, the harvest of years of delighted browsing and research into the lore of the East, contain the germ of many of his longer poems. They are indeed "literature in shorthand:"

> Knowledge? Know each other.
> Goodness? Love thy brother.

Here is a domestic one:

> This under the rose,
>   But it's true to the letter:
> The Man thinks he knows,
>   But the Woman knows better.

[13] Arthur Guiterman in the "Foreword" to *Betel Nuts*.

And then in the philosophical vein, these two:

Avoid suspicion: When you're walking through
Your neighbor's melon patch, don't tie your shoe.

and

Be peaceful, yet prepared, for harm is quick.
A sheep will bite a man without a stick.

Paul Elder's books were fine editions, especially designed for gifts. *Betel Nuts'* narrow tan pages were
printed in brown with borders of oriental motif. The
end papers were of vivid red. In 1908 he brought out a
large and handsome *Guest Book;* and for this great tome,
Arthur wrote glowing, warm-hearted verses to head
each page. The different parts of the house were repre-
sented as greeting the new arrival thus:

The Door

A faithful Door I stand, both strong and stout
To keep all Good within, all Ill without.
You knock. I open wide with right good will
While hearts that love you open wider still.

The Hearth

The Hearth am I, the deep heart of the dwelling,
A pleasant nook for ease and story-telling,
Where friendship's flame shall find a glad renewal
While mirth and kindly chat supply the fuel.

The Lamp

Sit, Bachelor Guest, within my rosy glow,
And ponder on a saw that thou shouldst know:
A house without a wife, poor lonely wight,
Is like a lanthorn left without a light.

The Hammock

I've heard them say that spoke as though they knew,
For one, I'm comfort, but I'm bliss for two.

As an adviser for Paul Elder's publishing house, Arthur's work ranged from getting up the company's catalogue to preparing special editions of *Sonnets from the Portuguese* and *The Literal Omar*. At the age of thirty-seven, he was fairly well established as a free-lance writer. But with his natural reticence and modesty, it is doubtful whether anything else could have proved such a spur to the poet's work as his marriage did. Those who knew Vida and Arthur, and even those who met them only briefly, will always remember the radiant together-ness that surrounded them. The tender references to Vida that appear again and again in Arthur's poetry are a living testament of the happiness they shared for almost thirty-four years. He paints an appreciative portrait in the lyric, "My Wife": [14]

Direct as lightning, brave as day
And clear-eyed as a star,

[14] *Lyric Laughter*, p. 120.

With plume aloft she goes her way
Serene where dragons are.

Like Roman roads her pathways run
Without a single bend;
Whenever something must be done
It's done, and that's the end.

Should any problems still persist
In clutching at her hem,
She simply says, "You don't exist!"
And that's the end of *them.*

I, far behind, with stumbling stops
Collect from sundry holes
The trifles that she lightly drops
Careering toward her goals.

A gay picture of their early adventures in housekeeping up on Washington Heights, is given in "At Number Eleven:" [15]

I think of it now as our corner of Heaven —
The little apartment at Number Eleven!
How boldly we leased it, without one misgiving!
How laughingly challenged the Problems of Living!
Rejecting all counsel, and scorning the censure
That elders bestowed on our reckless adventure,
Like two merry children we played at housekeeping—
And you did the dusting and I did the sweeping.

No palace was ever so tastefully furnished,
Nor ever was silver more ardently burnished.

[15] *Death and General Putnam and 101 Other Poems,* p. 154.

Our kitchen was cleanly beyond a suspicion;
The table and chair in my study were Mission;
A Chippendale desk was your chiefest of treasures,
And few were our worries, and simple our pleasures;
Not even the dishes were ever too trying,
For I did the washing and you did the drying.

We labored, we sorrowed, we triumphed together;
We mapped our own life-path, regardless of whether
Our course was the same that the world was pursuing,
For little we bothered what others were doing.
And now we have servants, and needs to employ them,
And manifold comforts, and well we enjoy them —
But we were the blithest of wedded beginners
When I got the breakfasts and you cooked the dinners.

Simple pleasures always appealed to the Guitermans.
Although they liked living in the city, they took every
opportunity to get into the country. Their friend, Stanley Isaacs, loving the outdoors as Arthur did, almost
every week-end organized tramping parties into the
Ramapos or out to Westchester. Stanley, who was later
to become President of the Borough of Manhattan,
showed his leadership then by planning these outings
in detail. His convictions and ideals were much like
Arthur's. Both believed in the value of outdoor exercise,
and they took to heart Theodore Roosevelt's advice,
"Do not pray for *easy* lives." Stanley's friends used to
tease him by saying that if his pack grew too light on
the way, he would put a few stones in it, or carry his

little daughter on his shoulder, in order to increase his burden for his soul's health!

It was shortly after his marriage that Arthur invented the Rhymed Reviews which became a feature of the old *Life* magazine for more than twenty years, and which were imitated by others. He took a current novel, told its story succinctly, and summed up in a stanza or a phrase his opinion of it. The first book of all that he treated was *The Inner Shrine* which appeared anonymously. The rhymed review began and ended thus:[16]

> Diane, though rather prone to flirt,
>   Was still so pure that none could doubt her
> Until a Marquis whom she'd hurt
>   Invented naughty tales about her.

> *   *   *

> The style is good, the plot is lame,
>   The moral standard's rather shady;
> The author does not sign his name —
>   Which proves that she's a perfect lady.

He could in a phrase take the wind from the sails of an exponent of weak philosophy, as he did when he discussed "How to Be a Yogi":[17]

> In Hindustan, that favored land,
>   True Yogis thrive like water cresses
> Beside a brook in August, and —
>   You know how Hindustan progresses!

[16] *Life*, August 12, 1909.
[17] *Life*, April 21, 1910.

Or he could laugh at the author whose characters are always of a type:

Simon the Jester [18]

BY WILLIAM J. LOCKE

I guess I'll make a Key to Locke:
  His Hero, simple or discerning
But always kindly, keeps a stock
  Of epigrams and facile learning.

His Heroine with bronze-gold hair
  And fervid heart that scorns conventions
Pops in from almost anywhere
  And trusts the Hero's good intentions.

He hides his love. She runs away.
  (This plot, of course, has variations.)
They meet again one happy day,
  And wed despite unequal stations.

The most widely appreciated and quoted of the reviews was that of Robert Hichens' *Bella Donna*,[19] which climaxed the story of the poisonous lady with these verses:

They met on shadowed desert scaurs,
  Baroudi's tent the couple screening.

" *   *   *   *   *   * "

(Observe I quote these little stars;
  Let Mr. Hichens clear their meaning.)

[18] *Life*, June 23, 1910.
[19] *Life*, December 9, 1909.

He dropped a hint; she snatched it up.
    With powdered lead in rank solution
She dosed her husband's coffee-cup
    And would have wrecked his constitution.

But ere the fatal work was done
    Appeared that heaven-sent physician,
The famous Doctor Isaacson,
    A Sherlock Holmes for intuition,

To spoil the game. With little ruth,
    He rent her sweet, angelic cover;
So Bella Donna owned the truth
    And fled by night to join her lover.

He cast her off. In blinded haste,
    Before the birds began to twitter,
She staggered far across the waste —
    I hope to God a lion bit her.

With the Rhymed Reviews, Letters to the Literati, and Impudent Interviews — all published in *Life* — he established the Arthur Guiterman habit among his readers. While he continued doing occasional work on the staffs of the *Woman's Home Companion* and the *Literary Digest*, his poems were appearing more and more often. Practically every American magazine welcomed his work at one time or another. "Graduates" of the *Youth's Companion* and *St. Nicholas* remained loyal followers when they rediscovered his verses in the *Saturday Evening Post*, *Scribner's*, *Harper's*, or the *Bookman*. He was one of the earliest contributors to the *New Yorker*, and

40

for eighteen years his warm humanity and sparkling wisdom seasoned the pages of that magazine, the last two contributions appearing after his death.

On Washington's birthday in 1910, the first meeting of what was to become the Poetry Society of America was held, and Edward Wheeler, editor of *Current Literature*, was chosen as president. Those early gatherings, at the National Arts Club, were lively ones, complete with ructions and fireworks; but the criticism was stimulating and the general effect good. It was there that Arthur first overcame his shyness and forced himself to get to his feet and speak, in the embarrassing silence that sometimes immediately followed the reading of a poem. During the years when free and imagist verse was the vogue, his voice demanding clarity and music was to be heard crying out in the wilderness of vague thought. Evidently, a majority of the members agreed with him, for they elected him president in 1925, and he ruled the meetings until 1927. It was during his administration, in 1926, that the Society, getting tired of providing a free show for the members of the Club, moved from the National Arts to more private quarters in the Roosevelt birthplace. Arthur believed the Poetry Society of America should be as truly national as its name indicated, and he welcomed his western friends, Lew Sarett and John Neihardt when they visited New York. He had a deep admiration for their poetry, for John Hall Wheelock's work, and for that of Harold

Pulsifer with whom he formed a lifelong friendship.

He also belonged for a while to a group of writers, editors, and artists who called themselves The Vagabonds and who met once a week at luncheon for discussion or to hear an invited speaker. Many of Arthur's poems appeared first in *The Bang*, the little magazine printed by The Vagabonds. Organized by some of the *Literary Digest's* staff, the club attracted interesting men. Among them were Leon Dabo, Theodore Dreiser, Walter Alden Dyer, Arthur T. Vance, Edward Wheeler; and Herman Rosenthal, head of the Slavonic Department of the New York Public Library, whose great wisdom and tolerant understanding of life appealed especially to Arthur. There were also two members who rejoiced in the refreshing names of Lemon and Seltzer. And somehow or other, George Sylvester Viereck got into the club. When he proved unpopular, no one knew how to get rid of him, for the rules had no provision for expelling a member. The problem was solved by disbanding the club and immediately reorganizing it — without Viereck!

In 1912, Arthur Guiterman was asked by the School of Journalism of New York University to teach verse writing. In this class, the first of its kind, he instructed many beginners as well as poets of promise like Mary Carolyn Davies and Elias Lieberman. When Arthur was asked in 1942 to name his favorite poems of patriotism, he concluded the list with these words: "And last, a poem that I cannot read without a catch in my throat, "I Am an American," by Elias Lieberman." [20]

As a result of his teaching experience, or of the time he spent reviewing slim volumes of verse for the *Outlook*, Arthur drew up a series of "Don'ts for Young Poets," of which this is perhaps the most characteristic admonition:

"Don't think of any class of work that you feel moved to do as either beneath you or above you."

There is plenty of evidence of the gifts of enjoyment that Vida and Arthur brought to each other. Speaking of his wife in a brief, autobiographical sketch,[21] he wrote: "She is the enterprising and adventurous member of the family who insists on foreign travel, airplane trips and things like that, while all I ask is a mountain, a forest, a lake, a river, a tennis court and a quiet study."

In 1915, they took their first sea trip together. They went on a liner on its maiden voyage through the Panama Canal to California. There they visited the two expositions and enjoyed the little one at San Diego, with its unbelievably blue skies and silken banners, much more than the mammoth one at San Francisco. They went on by train to Glacier, where they had their first experience of climbing on ice, Vida declaring that their guide had

[20] *Philadelphia Record*, April 12, 1942.
[21] *Saturday Evening Post*, August 18, 1928.

the horniest hand in the world. After Lake Louise and Banff, they returned to New York by way of Toronto and Montreal, stopping at Canadian Pacific hotels that all seemed to be called The Queen, The Alexandria, or The Victoria. All of their trips were to combine mountain climbing with the more conventional sight-seeing. New York remained their legal residence, and the poet's devotion to his city was deep and steadfast in his blood; but it never seemed strange to him that one who was at home in a Gotham apartment could be equally at home — and more deeply content — fishing a trout stream in Maine or climbing Katahdin.

That same year, 1915, *The Laughing Muse*, the first collection of Arthur's verse since the proverbs, appeared. In speaking of the work he did next, he said, "Then, although pigeonholed as a humorist, I went off on a tangent — as I have, time after time — and wrote a book of *Ballads of Old New York*. Collecting and publishing legends is a thankless task, at least in a city like New York where the modern has so completely deafened out the old that few New Yorkers realize what historically interesting ground they walk upon.

"The *Ballads* went the round of all the publishers. One firm almost took it — but did not quite dare assume the risk. . . . Later, after Harper's had brought out two volumes of my lighter verse, I offered them this same collection of historical ballads which they had turned down before. But this time the only question was in what form it should be brought out, a de luxe edition or a less expensive one."

Ballads of Old New York, beautifully illustrated, and *Chips of Jade* appeared in 1920, and were followed by *A Ballad Maker's Pack* in 1921. *The Mirthful Lyre* had come out in 1918. After *The Light Guitar* appeared in 1923, Harper's brought out a uniform edition of the three books of light verse.[22] Writing of the collection, Charles Wharton Stork said:[23]

"Unlike most facile versifiers, Arthur Guiterman writes mainly when he has something worth saying, relegating his technical skill to its proper place as an ornament, not as an end in itself. He wants first of all to express a thought and only secondarily to express it neatly.... A poet with his message at once of sanity and of sympathy, with his mastery of whatever material he chooses, above all with his sparkle and often felicity of style stands very nearly as good a chance with posterity as did Robert Herrick."

The section of *The Light Guitar* called "The Lyric Baedeker" [24] might stand as an itinerary for at least the high lights of the Guitermans' first European trip in 1921. Their ship docked at Glasgow, and the poem about that city contains these lines:

[22] *The Laughing Muse, The Mirthful Lyre, The Light Guitar.*

[23] Literary Review, *New York Evening Post*, May 16, 1925.

[24] Pages 78-94.

45

But drab is the town as a shawl-hooded crone,
And dreary and cold with a chill all its own.
You ask them for bread and they give you a scone,
     In Glasgow.

Then the lyrics take us on to Edinburgh, where

The castle is a gallant keep and one you're bound to view;
    A military pensioner will kindly take you through,
Rehearsing inexhaustibly the plots and counterplots
    That made it insalubrious for Mary Queen of Scots.

After a stay in London, Vida and Arthur spent a month
in tramping through north Devon, and the verses tell us
that

    The maidens of Devon, if all that they seem
    Are made out of strawberries, sugar and cream.

The Guitermans flew in an open cockpit plane from
London to Paris — a flight which in that era was still
rather a stunt. They had the two seats in the very front
of the plane — even in front of the pilot; and there was
nothing between them and the universe but a wind-
shield. The roar of the motor and the wind made conversation impossible, but sharing such an exciting new
experience without speaking to each other was equally
impossible for Vida and Arthur. Fortunately, they
found that the sign before them, printed in two languages, warning passengers not to throw anything out
of the plane, contained practically every letter of the
alphabet. By pointing to letters, they were able to spell
out the words they had to say to each other!

In Paris they found flags flying and people dancing
on the sidewalks, and suddenly realized it was July 14,
Bastille Day. Of that city, Arthur wrote:

> The Taxicabs of Paris
> Malevolently squeal,
> They leap around the corner
> Upon a single wheel;
> It's up to you to dodge them,
> For if you dare to fail,
> And get yourself run over,
> They put you into jail.

Tramping in the Swiss Alps with packs on their backs
was a happy experience for a mountain-loving man and
his travel-loving wife, as the poem, "The Alps," clearly
shows:

> Where the foaming Visp is born
> From the snows of Matterhorn,
> We whose feet had spurned the shale
> Up Katahdin's wilder trail,
> Bound again the rover's pack,
> Took once more the gypsy track.

> Loose of bonds of time or plan,
> Far and free our roadway ran:
> Threading valleys boulder-strown
> Past the icy birth of Rhone,
> Past the glacier's mighty mass,
> Through the mists of Furka Pass,
> Cleaving hills of glossy pine —
> Hills that nursed the infant Rhine,
> Over Julier's height went we
> And down the Alps to Italy.

Friendly greetings, easy slumbers,
Cowbells chanting golden numbers,
Glacial reaches calm and chilly
Where the marmot whistles shrilly,
Upland pastures fresh and sunny,
Noonday halts to bread and honey,
Plunging river, azure dome —
Oh, my mountains, you are home!

In Venice, it was the "shambling, gambling, rambling, scrambling, gondolling gondolier" who was immortalized. "The Lyric Baedeker" concludes with

At home I never stare and wonder,
For that would be a social blunder;
But Romans prize their city's stories
And flock to scan her ancient glories;
So when in Rome, as duly bid,
I did the way the Romans did.

The year before the European trip is memorable because it introduced Vida and Arthur to Arlington, Vermont, the lovely mountain village that was to occupy such an important place in their hearts. They were familiar with New England, for they had spent many summers deep in the Maine woods and tramping the White Mountains. But somehow they had missed Vermont. As Arthur's poetry became widely known, he was more and more in demand as a lecturer. Never a formalist in any way, he had a talent for being himself on the lecture platform, and his audiences felt the charm of his genuine sincerity. In the summer of 1920, Mrs.

Halley Gilchrist, President of the Poetry Society of Southern Vermont, wrote to ask him if he would speak and read for that group. There was to be no remuneration beyond expenses, but it was the right time of year to go to the country. Mrs. Gilchrist invited the Guitermans to spend the week-end at her home in Arlington. They promptly fell in love with the little town that lies quietly in the valley between the Green Mountains and the Taconics. There they met Robert Frost, and Dorothy Canfield Fisher whose friendship they always treasured and to whom Arthur later dedicated the "Mountain Village" section of one of his books.[25] They were so completely enchanted by Arlington that they returned in September of the same year and spent almost a month at a farm, taking walks up to Kelly Stand's deserted village, visiting Red Mountain's cave, driving with friends around Dorset Hollow, and climbing mountains to get a better view of the gorgeous autumn coloring.

This was the beginning of an attraction which meant so much to the Guitermans that they returned again and again to Arlington and finally bought a home there. Nor was the affection one-sided. Arlington liked them, too. In 1928, Dorothy Canfield Fisher invited them to spend the summer in the south wing of Brick House. The house, formerly the home of Aunt Mattie (Miss Martha Canfield), now belonged to Mrs. Fisher. The

[25] *Gaily the Troubadour*, E. P. Dutton & Co. (New York, 1936).

north wing served as a library, and the main body of the house was used as a community center, but the South Wing contained compact living quarters to which Mrs. Fisher invited special summer guests. Vida and Arthur were going to Spain that year — a trip which included walking expeditions in Majorca and the Pyrenees, but they got back in time to accept the invitation from late July until the end of September. Their pleasure in the little home in the heart of Arlington is shown in "Brick House": [26]

We had more than enough with a roof overhead
And a room with a desk and a room with a bed,
For we bathed in the brook in the glow of the dawn
And we cooked on the porch what we ate on the lawn.

There were vines on the wall, there were flowers in the
     garth
And when it was chill there were logs for the hearth;
And the dog had a bone and the cat had a mouse
In the little South Wing of the old Brick House.

So happily did the Guitermans fit into the Vermont landscape that Dorothy Canfield renewed her invitation year after year in spite of their protests.

"Some summer," Vida warned their hostess, "you'll want to invite someone else to Brick House, and you'll feel you can't do it because of us."

But Dorothy promised that she would be perfectly

[26] *Ibid.*, p. 137.

frank if a time should come when she needed Brick House, and the guests came back every summer until 1933. Since Mrs. Fisher would not let them pay rent, they had satisfied themselves by giving presents to the house itself—putting a dormer in the loft of the carriage-house to make guest quarters there, building on a bath-room, etc. In 1933, the town of Arlington explained to Mrs. Fisher that it was difficult to get money enough to buy coal for the Community House during the long winters, and it would help greatly if they could rent the South Wing the year round in order to pay the fuel bill.

Strangely enough, this was the same year that Arthur was told by his doctor that cold weather and blustery winds were bad for his arterial condition. Since he was ordered south for the winters, the Guitermans decided to give up their big Madison Avenue apartment in New York, for it seemed extravagant to keep it if they were to be away so much of the year. It was then that they found Hillhouse, quietly overlooking Arlington from the north, definitely a part of the village, and yet because of its elevation, somehow separate. Seven acres of land went with the house. They rented the place for three years, moved all their furniture up, and began making it their own. When in the fall of 1937 they decided to buy Hillhouse, each was trying to close the deal as a surprise for the other's birthday. Arthur told guests proudly, "Wherever we live, Vida makes improvements. She did so much to this place that we *had* to buy it." Although

in the early days of their marriage she had done pro-
fessional decorating, her later interest centered in hand-
lettering and illuminating. Besides the beautiful books
and wall-pieces that she made for others, Vida lettered
and illustrated with her most exquisite skill her favorites
among her husband's poems.

But it was not the added fireplace and chimney, the
extra bathrooms, or the modernized guest wing that
wooed them into owning Hillhouse. The wooded grove
north of the house was the scene of many a picnic;
Vida's garden was growing lovelier each year; their own
meadow, stretching up to the edge of the woods, pro-
vided a good beginning for a walk; and then there was
the view. Hillhouse faces west and looks squarely at
the scene that is depicted on the official seal of the
state of Vermont. The seal shows two mountains with
a pine tree between them, and a cow grazing under the
tree. The mountains and the very top of the pine face
Hillhouse, and an obliging cow often crosses the meadow
at the foot of the mountains. The poem, "Hillhouse,"
written while they were still only renters, was a sort of
prophecy that they would have to own the place:[27]

> The spirit of the hills shall bless
>   This home of ours;
> The elves of pond and stream shall dress
>   Our fields with flowers;
> The Muses shall not hurry past,

[27] *Death and General Putnam and 101 Other Poems*, page 156.

> But harbor near
> Where Peace abides, and Hope shall cast
>   Her anchor here;
> Young Pan shall make our woodland blithe
>   With nymph and faun,
> And Time shall only use his scythe
>   To mow our lawn.

Their first southern migration was to Winter Park, Florida — a delightful community they had discovered when Arthur had been asked to give a poetry course at Rollins College in 1931. They made many friends there, and the residents chuckled over the Guiterman verses that described the cultural life:[28]

> In many a town of lesser sort
>   You'll hear a constant swishing-swashing,
> For people's means of self-support
>   Is taking in each other's washing.

> But here where cultured folk reside
>   (Or so my simple soul conjectures),
> Our time is chiefly occupied
>   With sitting through each other's lectures.

Afterwards, they varied their winters by going sometimes to California, sometimes to the West Indies, but oftenest to Florida.

It was Rollins College which awarded the degree of Doctor of Literature to Arthur in 1940, and the citation spoke of the distinction that was his in giving "cheer

[28] "Winter Park, Florida," *Gaily the Troubadour*, p. 82.

to a generation of people," in lightening "the cares of a troubled world with laughter," and in showing "that humor may be rich in humanity and sympathy." Many years before, Arthur had been elected to membership in Phi Beta Kappa. It was not the custom of his own college to confer honorary degrees, but during the years he was twice selected by the City College of New York Alumni Association for awards — the Conspicuous Service medal and the Townsend Harris medal — both in recognition of his contributions to the world of letters and the world of men.

It would be difficult to make a list of the friends who held important places in Arthur's life. Even those who met him casually felt close to him, for he could be so wholeheartedly outgiving that a five-minute conversation with him could mean more than hours of talk with others. His publisher said, "It was a delight to discuss anything with him — even a contract." Through their Valentines, composed by Arthur and lettered and decorated by Vida, for nearly twenty years they kept in touch with a wide circle. There is no adequate way to convey Vida's decorations in words, but all of the Valentines have the unique Guiterman quality of this one, sent in 1940:

> Love is no stuff to gather dust on shelves:
> The more we give the more we have ourselves.
> So all our love we send to you, and then
> Still more we'll have to send to you again.

For two decades he enjoyed the friendship of Walter Brickner, the surgeon; and it was after Dr. Brickner's death in 1930 that he wrote "For All Who Mourn": [29]

> That he was dear to you so many a year
>   But darkens your distress.
> Would you he were less worthy and less dear
>   That you might grieve the less?
>
> He was a golden font that freely poured
>   What goldenly endures,
> And though that font be gone, its bounty, stored
>   And treasured, still is yours.
>
> The Past is deathless. Souls are wells too deep
>   To spend their purest gains.
> All that he gave to you is yours to keep
>   While memory remains.
>
> Who never had and lost, forlorn are they
>   Far more than you and I
> Who had and have. Grudge not the price we pay
>   For love that cannot die.

Another close friend was Edmund Pearson, whose studies of actual murders were written with a historian's accuracy and a novelist's ability to characterize and describe. After Vida and Arthur met Edmund and his charming wife Sally, they made a congenial foursome for Sunday walks along the old aqueduct road from Van Cortlandt to Scarsdale, where they would lunch

[29] *Death and General Putnam and 101 Other Poems*, p. 71.

late and luxuriously and return home by train. The Pearsons were their comrades for many years, and Edmund's death in 1937 was a great blow to them. Dr. Ira Wile was another good companion. After an evening with the Wiles, the Pearsons, and the Guitermans, when the meeting of keen minds and rich personalities had made the conversation a memorable delight, I asked Arthur why all conversation couldn't be so enjoyable, and he said, "Because there aren't many people in the world like the Pearsons and the Wiles." Never a "joiner," Arthur belonged to few literary organizations. To the Authors' League and the Poetry Society, he gave his time freely; but he had no taste for confining his social life to an "artistic" group. Hackett was an actor; Albert Heymann, a business man; Walter Brickner, a surgeon; Stanley Isaacs, a lawyer; Edmund Pearson, a writer; Ira Wile, a psychiatrist; and they were all close to Arthur's heart.

In 1926, I come into the Guiterman's story ever so slightly, in a manner that illustrates Arthur's helpfulness to would-be writers. I was a senior in a Pittsburgh high school and a Guiterman fan. My English teacher spoke of Arthur as a master of metrical composition, as one who knew all there was to know about the technique of poetry. At this time, Arthur was President of the Poetry Society and of the Authors' League Fellowship. Besides the duties of these offices and his writing and lecturing, he took every possible opportunity to speak up for clarity and meaning and to condemn obscurity and vague "self-expression" in poetry. His time was filled to overflowing. But when I wrote to him, he was not too busy to answer. I told him I wanted to be a poet, and two days later I had a reply which I carried proudly to school to share with my English class. He warned me against putting all my eggs in one basket, spoke of the advisability of trying all kinds of writing until one found what he could do best, and criticized kindly the verses I had sent him. His letter ended, "And although you will never believe it, seventeen is really very young."

That prompt answer was typical of the man. When someone wrote to him for advice, he gave it immediately. Though he had little patience with literary pretenders, it was impossible for him to ignore any serious inquiry. I treasured the contact with him so greatly that I kept on writing to him, about once a year, to tell him about some little personal triumph or setback and to ask advice about my own writing which was embryonic, or at best, adolescent. His letters were a good mirror of his personality. In criticism, he did not indulge in false praise; but he was never cruel or sharp. He showed his genuine friendliness by adding some word of what he and Vida were doing; and so I knew that they went to Spain in 1928, and that in 1932 they reached Arlington "by way of Holland, Germany, Austria, and Colorado!"

Though I had never seen either of them, I dreamed of going to New York some day and meeting them.

When I did go in 1934, to take a summer course at Columbia, I was disappointed to find that they were already in Vermont. Arthur wrote that they would certainly look me up if they should return to the city during the summer, and I was resigning myself to disappointment, when there came a letter from Vida, inviting me to Hillhouse for a week-end. Her brother, she said, drove up very often and would be glad to take me. I wrote an ecstatic acceptance, and the week-end came and went in a haze of pure delight. In two days, I met Vida's brother, Connecticut, Massachusetts, the Berkshires, Vermont, Dorothy Canfield Fisher, and my adored Guitermans — all for the first time — and I went home in a state of inspired happiness that has never quite left me. To this day, I marvel at the generous impulse that prompted Vida to invite me, sight unseen, to their home.

Within a year or so, I became a sort of unofficial member of the Guiterman family, sometimes known as The Child. Though I was rather old for the title, I enjoyed it very much, as I did the privilege of being close to their hearts and minds.

Although the parallel probably never occurred to him, Arthur's life was much like that of his hero, Theodore Roosevelt, in that he developed himself from a rather frail boyhood to an active, athletic manhood. The winds of the out-of-doors blew through his life and his poetry,

and he was never happier than when he was climbing
a mountain or setting out on a trail through the woods.
To see a woodchuck, a rabbit, or a deer, changed an
ordinary walk into an adventure. When in later years
his activity was limited because of his heart condition,
he resented it deeply. His natural impulse was to strike
out uphill, and his poem, "Hills," expresses the philosophy of his thought and action: [30]

> I never loved your plains,
>   Your gentle valleys,
> Your drowsy country lanes
>   And pleachèd alleys.
>
> I want my hills! — the trail
>   That scorns the hollow.
> Up, up the ragged shale
>   Where few will follow,
>
> Up, over wooded crest
>   And mossy boulder
> With strong thigh, heaving chest
>   And swinging shoulder,
>
> So let me hold my way,
>   By nothing halted,
> Until, at close of day
>   I stand exalted
>
> High on my hills of dream,
>   Dear hills that know me.

[30] *Scribner's*, July, 1915 and *Death and General Putnam and 101
Other Poems*, p. 19.

And then, how fair will seem
The lands below me,

How pure at vesper-time
The far bells chiming!
God, give me hills to climb
And strength for climbing!

And yet he was perfectly at home in New York.
Knowing the city's history as few natives bother to
know it, he loved to walk in Inwood or Tryon and point
out the strategy of battles that had been fought there.
He was proud of New York and had a deep affection
for it. Perhaps the secret of his diversity is that he was
simply at home in the world. He once wrote: [31]

"By nature I am a stick-in-the-mud, well satisfied with
what I have tested and found good; but the lady who
married me has a way of saying, 'Just think of all the
places we haven't seen!' And she sometimes succeeds
in dragging me away, groaning and protesting, to
France, Spain, Switzerland, Italy, and other foreign
parts where they don't speak my language and disdain
my attempts to speak theirs. What I really enjoy are
our many excursions deep into our own woods and
mountains; and I recall with special delight six glorious
weeks of tramping over the high trails of the Rockies
with our packs and fishing-rods."

In spite of the "groaning and protesting," he had the

[31] *Classmate*, May 12, 1932. Methodist Board of Education (Nashville, Tenn.).

happy faculty of enjoying his experiences to the full.
When a newspaper asked him to tell about the moment
of his life which gave him the greatest thrill, he replied,
"At first, I was inclined to choose the moment of breaking the tape at the finish of a hundred yards' dash, or
that of shooting a winning goal in ice hockey, because
there is nothing more exhilarating than the sense of
physical fitness and power combined with exaltation
that comes in athletic victories. And then I remembered
a beautiful June morning on the cliffs of north Devon,
looking down on Sillery Sands and the waters of the
Bristol Channel, when a skylark rose from the gorse at
my feet and for the first time I heard that miraculous
song. Oliver Herford had said to me before I left for
England: 'I'd like to see your face when you first hear
a skylark,' and then I knew what he meant. But I think
that I had a still higher moment last August in the
Colorado Rockies. Six of us had ridden up from the
Conejos, sometimes along old sheep trails, sometimes
breaking our way through groves of aspen, to a ridge
about 12,000 feet high. Below us was the beautiful
valley of the Conejos River; above the mountains on
the opposite side a storm was blowing toward us from
New Mexico, the lightning playing through the black
clouds; and as we galloped along the edge of the splendid
cliff, over our heads in the clear sunlight wheeled two
great eagles."

His enjoyment of life naturally made him a good

companion. Every summer in Vermont we had an important date to go canoeing on the Battenkill. Traffic isn't expected on a quiet mountain stream, but a team of horses once drove a wagonload of hay across the river directly in front of our canoe. When you went anywhere with Arthur, things happened! Outdoors or in, he was fun to be with. Though he punned rarely, he could not resist a good one. Looking at a newspaper picture of the Duchess of Windsor presiding over a tea table, Arthur said with a sigh and a twinkle, "She never reigns, but she pours." He always managed to give the most ordinary observation a twist of his own. When conquerors and conquests were being discussed, he said, "History repeats herself so fast she practically stutters." In mentioning the interviews he so often gave to newspaper people and students, and of the difficulty of being confronted with questions demanding immediate answers, he spoke of the phenomenon of "improvising lifelong convictions." When he was trying to recall a name that had slipped from his memory, he said, "I haven't even a mental whisper of it." His fund of information was amazing, and it extended beyond the realms of history and literature into nature lore, astronomy, and almost every field of human knowledge. His older brother once said in simple tribute, "Arthur knows everything." And to hear him tell a story was to see it all happening before your eyes, for his words gave life and color to all he said.

His correspondence was voluminous. Of course, there were autograph-seekers, but more often people wrote him to express appreciation of his work — usually of some particular poem. Those in sorrow thanked him for "Mizpah" [32] and "For All Who Mourn"; and the light verse, too, moved readers to write to the author. One woman said, "Whenever a poem of yours appears in the *Saturday Evening Post* you can rest assured, I read it. I've sent your latest one, entitled 'Outdoor Furniture' to my son who is somewhere in Australia." Another wrote, "I am a waitress twenty years old. It seems to me that, more than any other contemporary poet, you are able to picture many different moods skilfully, beauty, humor, pathos, and all the rest." A schoolgirl informed him, "I am memorizing 'Strictly Germ-Proof.' I will surely get a good laugh when I recite it." Younger fellow poets discussed his writing and theirs, and school children naïvely called on him for help in their compositions. A girl named Peggy began her letter, "I hope you don't think me an old bore, but in my English class . . . we have to look up authors for our 6 wks. test. I have to look up your life and I cannot find any interesting details in the *old* encyclopedias we have . . . I have to give my report on you the 21st of this month so please, if you're not to busy, will you answer this right away?" A prompt answer was evidently the youngsters' usual need, for another said, "Due to limited time it is neces-

[32] *Death and General Putnam and 101 Other Poems*, p. 109.

sary that your reply be immediate, please." But a Washington boy, after listing his questions, offered information in return: "I suppose you wonder what sort of a country these Western States are. We have a good deal of rain in the winter but have good weather during the summer season. The most important industries are farming, fishing and lumber industries — when the men are not on a strike." An English class wrote simply to wish him a happy birthday; and a man from Georgia, asking where he might find "House Blessing," made this interesting offer: "I tell you what, you send me the poem and I will send you some Pecans or Peanuts, whichever you prefer."

He was especially successful in making friends with children. His genuineness and lack of pretense or pose made them feel at home with him, and they accepted him as their equal. At one of the annual pet shows that Vida instituted on the lawn of Hillhouse, a little girl came to him sobbing, "Mr. Guiterman! Mr. Guiterman! My kitten has something in her eye!" Arthur administered first aid to the kitten, at the same time consoling the little girl by reminding her that *she* had often had something in her eye and it hadn't proved fatal.

The Guitermans' own cats were the source of many a poem. Arthur was fond of all animals, and could never understand the animosity that dog lovers sometimes feel for cats, and vice versa. He and Vida did not keep a dog because of their moving from place to place, but it was easy to acquire kittens in Arlington and then give them away at the end of the summer. Miss Purrington was their first; and when it became evident that two kittens together were more than twice as much fun as one alone, they had such pairs as Adelina Catti and Catti-Gazazza, Horsefeathers and Applesauce, Malt and Hops, Catnip and Catkin.

But speaking only of the poet's gentle kindness and deep enjoyment of living would give a one-sided picture. He was painfully sensitive, and an unpleasant voice or an inane conversationalist could send him off to a state of aloof quiet which was partly protective and partly the result of early shyness. When he was tired or annoyed, he crawled into his shell. Also, he had strong convictions and never hesitated to speak up for them. He said once, "You have no idea how many times a peace-loving person like me can be forced to get out and fight." When anything seemed to him *wrong*, he said so clearly and decisively. As early as 1901, he wrote:[33]

> The time is past for lives of gentle heart
>   And pallid sinlessness and cloistered ease.
> He sins, today, who fails to bear his part
>   In putting right the bitter wrong he sees.

He was singularly consistent in that attitude throughout his life, and it is significant that the *Herald Tribune*

[33] "The Boss," *New York Times*, January 13, 1901.

received from him on the very day before his death the lines protesting the appointment of "Plenipotentiary Paving-Stone Flynn" [34] as an ambassador. In three wars, his poetry took up his country's cause; and long before Pearl Harbor, the weapon of his pen had been turned against the Axis while his voice spoke in earnest warning to fellow-Americans. As far back as 1937, he wrote:[35]

To Japan

It is not war; your bombs that have no ruth
   Rain down on peaceful townsman, farmer, herder.
This is not war. For once you speak the truth:
   'Tis only murder.

On almost every important issue that came before the people during his lifetime, it is possible to find his view expressed in verse. His "Blessing on the Woods," [36] which was rejected by several editors before he despaired of selling it and gave it to F. P. A. for publication in his column, *The Conning Tower*, became a litany for conservationists and was reprinted many times.

In less important ways, too, his writing was effective in calling attention to a need for action. His rhymed "Letters" in the *New Yorker* not only prompted Al Smith to turn off the ugly red on the tower of the Empire

---

[34] "Paving Stones," *New York Herald Tribune*, January 14, 1943.
[35] *New York Herald Tribune*, September 29, 1937.
[36] *Death and General Putnam and 101 Other Poems*, p. 22.

State[37] but also succeeded in winning a bath and complete rejuvenation for the Lady of the Plaza, the Pulitzer Memorial Fountain.[38]

Although his early work included almost every known form of writing, it was natural that his contribution should be poetic when he entered the field of the drama and opera. In 1933, he collaborated with Lawrence Langner in a rhymed adaptation of Molière's *School for Husbands*, produced by the Theatre Guild. His "metrical essay on collaboration,"[39] which appeared in the *Times* the day before the play opened in New York, begins thus:

Cried Lawrence Langner leaping from his lair,
Upon my shoulders, "Say! You know Molière?"
Said I, "Why, no; I never read the papers;
It sounds like shaving cream or asthma vapors."
"No, no! He scribbled plays in France," said Lawrence.
Said I, "You know the Stage is my abhorrence;
I don't read plays; besides, I must acknowledge,
I barely passed in languages at college."
Said Lawrence, "You've no better occupation,
So take this play and make a good translation.
Observe how easily the language flows;
And, since Molière disdained the bonds of prose,
You put it all in rhyme, the same as he did,

[37] "Letter to Mr. Smith," January 30, 1932 and note in "Talk of the Town," February 20, 1932.

[38] "Letter to Mr. Pulitzer," April 18, 1931 and "Letter to Mr. Guiterman," May 2, 1931.

[39] From Preface of *School for Husbands*.

been describing his own case in "Pierrot Explains Himself": [41]

> For song, I thank the birds; for mirth, the streams;
>   For tales, the wind that walks among the trees;
> For deeper lore, the world; for lovely dreams
>   I thank the moon, but thank far more than these
> My birth-star, twinkling, twinkling through the drift
>   Of broken cloud and filmy haze above
> The sleeping city, for the golden gift
>   Of humor which is laughter mixed with love.
> I win no laurels; such the schools bestow
>   Upon the solemn wise from whom I turn
> To laugh, which is not wise; and still I know
>   How well the wise may come to me and learn;—
> And here they come, the wise of all the schools,
> To me, the little brother of all fools!

"Laughter mixed with love" was his favorite definition of humor, and that particularly delightful brand of humor blossoms in abundance in his work. Though he could satirize neatly, there was never the slightest hint of meanness in anything he wrote or did. His turn of mind never betrayed him by letting him go over to the school of the sophisticates. (He once classified the world-weary, humorously cynical group as "sophisticates, sophisticats, and little sophistikittens.") Over a long period of years, he stands out in the field of American letters as one who was true to his own ideals in the matter of literary standards and taste, as well as in ways

[41] *Death and General Putnam and 101 Other Poems*, p. 51.

of thinking. In the era of disillusionment after the first World War, when patriotism was likely to be called chauvinism, and pacifism began to be a cult, he went on singing with passionate fervor of the honor and glory of his country's past, of the need to be ever watchful of that honor and glory. When he was asked to contribute a poem to some pacifistic organization, he said, "Saying that one loves peace is like saying one loves his mother. Who doesn't?" But it did not seem to him wise to put peace before everything else, and he never forgot the words of Theodore Roosevelt: "If I must choose between peace and righteousness, I choose righteousness."

Arthur's death came as he would have wished it — in line of duty. On the morning of January 11, 1943, he was on the way to the Twentieth Century Club in Pittsburgh to deliver a lecture on *Brave Laughter*. Because he felt it unpatriotic to take a cab in the midst of gasoline and rubber shortages, he had gone by streetcar from the hotel, and had walked from the car in a high wind. Before he reached the Club, he was stricken with a heart attack. The doorman, sent out to look for him, reached him as he collapsed the second time, and helped him into the Club, where Arthur insisted, "Just let me rest a few minutes, and then I can give my lecture." But the doctor who was called, ordered him to the hospital.

There he convinced the specialist that he would be
well enough by evening to take the train to Washington
where Vida was waiting for him to go on to Florida
for the rest of the winter. When he was told in the late
afternoon that it would be best for him to remain quietly
in bed for a few days, he frowned. The doctor said,
"This shouldn't bother the author of 'Death and General
Putnam.' "

Arthur said quickly, "Oh, it isn't *that*. It's the reservations I'm thinking of."

But the reservations were canceled, and Vida was
notified. Arthur spoke to her over the telephone, apolo-
gizing for being sick and for postponing their trip south,
and she told him she would be with him as soon as she
could get there. She was on the way when he died at
ten that night.

I was called at noon at the school where I was teaching,
and so I had the privilege of being with him all that
afternoon and evening. He was so exactly himself —
gentle, considerate, and thoughtful — that I could not
believe he was going to die. When I asked him where
he was when the first heart attack occurred, he said
simply, "Up on the hill," and it seems fitting that up
to the very end of his life, he should have been climbing.
Time and again, the theme of climbing comes into his
poetry. It is in the envoy to "The Eagle," which Arthur
spoke of as an expression of his philosophy; and in "Hills"
there is the prayerful climax:

> God, give me hills to climb
>   And strength for climbing.

In *A Poet's Proverbs,* he puts it this way:

> God's Road is all uphill,
>   But do not tire.
> Rejoice that we may still
>   Keep climbing higher.

He believed deeply in courage and in fighting to set right the wrongs of the world, he loved and rejoiced in the out-of-doors, he knew how to live and how to die, and he left the world a rich legacy of song and brave laughter.

ELEANOR GRAHAM

New York City
1943

WHERE THE ROAD
MIGHT LEAD

Men make a camp, a swarm of bees a comb;
Birds make a nest; a woman makes a home.

The beggar is lord of his dole,
The mouse is the king of his hole.

¶ Utility

What is the use of the frozen poles,
   The peaks of eternal snow,
The measureless spaces that call our souls
   And all that we yearn to know?

What is the use of a singing bird,
   The dew on the hawthorn spray,
A fragrance, a glory, a thought, a word,
   Or the child that was born today?

Weigher of worth, have you never sowed
   To prove what was in the seed,
Or eagerly followed an unmarked road
   To learn where the road might lead?

¶ Courage and Mirth

Twinborn, ye are, and of heavenly birth,
  Courage and Mirth.
Helpers of Man in his dolor and dearth,
Come to a desolate, humorless earth,
Strengthen and hearten the children of earth,
  Courage and Mirth!

❡ The Forerunners

The dauntless pioneers, the selfless starters
Of great reforms, derided, often martyrs,
The voices in our wildernesses, crying
Unheard the truths that now we hold undying,
The fighting prophets, they who through the ages
Have won no crowns, have borne with bitter wages,
The men before their time, the first who said it
And toiled for it and never had the credit,
I raise a monument, though not of stone,
To these, forgotten, unrevered, unknown.

꧁ Parable for Conquerors

Gordius of Phrygia wove the leathern thong
  Between his chariot pole and yoke to hold
The twain together in a knot so strong
  And intricate that oracles foretold
That he alone whose deftness should undo
  The twisted ligature might rule as lord
Of Asia. Alexander, one that knew
  No patience, clove the fastening with his sword
And seized dominion, but in youth he died,
  His empire with him. Tyrants come and go,
Cutters of knots that should have been untied,
  The knotted warp of human pain and woe.
Untanglers of our knots who find the cure
  Of ills by wisdom, leave what shall endure.

¶ The Victor

Our earth has borne them, ah, so many times,
These conquerors, their cruelties and crimes,
The triumphs of the brute, the gilded savage,
Oppression, broken pledges, murder, ravage,
Perversion of the glories of the brain
To basest uses!
        Over heaps of slain
How many haughty ones have rolled to bind
Their world in chains, then passed and left behind
The smolder of a brand, a saber's gleam,
The fading memory of an evil dream!
Vast empery they won, and winning, wrought
Prodigious villainies, yet all for nought;
Kind darkness covers Attila the bane
Of Europe, Alexander, Tamerlane,
Old Nimrod, Rameses and Genghis Khan;
Their might is nothingness, but Man goes on.
Faltering, stumbling, erring from the way,
Still Man toils onward toward the light of day;
And though to us his upward march seems slow,
With God it is not so.

¶ The Little, Bewildered People

In them through the world's confusion
    The urge of the race survives:
To work and to play, to rest and to love,
    To live out their simple lives;
To render to God and to Caesar
    The things that to each belong,
To hold their conviction of what is right,
    Their loathing of what is wrong.

Yet patiently, blindly, bravely,
    Unable to fathom why,
Poor pawns of a ruthless player,
    They suffer, they toil, they die.
Then give them a moment's pity,
    A prayer for their heartache, too,
The little, bewildered people
    Who do what they're told to do.

¶ Pilot

Around the headland's rugged brow,
    Beyond the hidden bar,
With steady hand I hold her bow
    Still pointing toward her star.

The seas are breaking fore and aft,
    Alee, the reef is near,
The stormwinds rage to sink the craft,
    But while she floats, I steer.

¶ The Veterans

What! As the end draws nigh
They would lay a wreath
On the battered crest,
Then, with the spear put by,
With the sword in sheath,
They would have us rest!

Rest? Is there time for rest
As the days grow few,
While our friends fall fast,
When we must strive our best
Since each deed we do
May be called our last?

Ye, that are young and strong,
With your paths untrod
May be idle a space;
We, who have lived this long
By the grace of God,
Must prove worthy His grace.

❡ Crossroads

Good-by, dear friend. Some day, I guess not when,
These pleasant hours shall know a glad rebirth;
The world is wide, yet we shall meet again,
For there are many crossroads on this earth.

And Death may not deny us time and place;
No skies between shall make our hope the worse;
The more the teeming stars, the vaster space,
The more the crossroads of the universe.

❡ Epitaph

Friends whom I loved to name,
    Know, should you mourn for me,
I, that was not, became;
    I, that am not, shall be.

¶ The Eternal Question

Dear little boy, there are well-schooled men
To answer "Who?" "Where?" "How?" and
   "When?"
Yet the wisest give but a vague reply
If you ask them "Why?"

There are tested facts, so the books declare,
In proof of Who, How, When and Where,
But we only guess with a doubtful sigh
At the question "Why?"

Why is there sin, why grief, why pain?
The ages ask, and they ask in vain;
So we seek, we dream till the day we die,
When we may know "Why."

¶ Sanctuary

Since now you must go
    To where your roads run,
Remember and know,
    My daughter, my son,
Whatever you do,
    Wherever you roam,
This door is for you,
    This house is your home.

❡ The Child

He cried for the moon; from the sky where she rolled
I plucked her for him, and he found her too cold.

He cried for the sun as he lay in his cot;
I gave her to him, and he found her too hot.

He wanted the earth for amusement or study;
I gave her to him, and he found her too muddy.

So, cloud, star, or lightning, I never denied,
But gave what he cried for the instant he cried.

How else could he learn that from bearing to dying
No gift that he'd cry for would prove worth the
    crying!

◗ Old Wives' Tale

Assyria, Persia, Egypt, Rome
   Knew Rapine's bitter aftermath
When pillared fane and golden dome
   Went down in red, barbaric wrath.

Still tyrants rage; defying Fate,
   Again, again and yet again
They sow the dragon's teeth of Hate
   And up spring hordes of vengeful men.

Then vaunt your conquests' cruel worth,
   Be deaf to all but servile cheers!
Your walls and towers shall crash to earth
   For they are built on blood and tears.

❡ Be a Good Sport

You've given up a thing or two
    That every free man cherishes;
What else should anybody do
    Till Hitlerism perishes?

Your taxes rise, your costs expand,
    Your little wealth diminishes;
Such private woes we'll have to stand
    Till Schickelgruber finishes.

You fear that yielding any rights
    Means liberty's demolishment;
Still, let's suspend internal fights
    Till Nazidom's abolishment.

The bull is in the china shop,
    So what a foolish mockery
To cry because his tamers drop
    And crack your bit of crockery!

¶ Inventors

Pay homage to the first who made a fire,
    Who bent and strung a bow, whose rugged art
Devised the wheel, whose passionate desire
    For utterance found symbols to impart
Both thought and spoken word! Brave pioneers,
    Battling with demons, demons of the storm,
The flood, the earthquake, through the desert years
    They cleared a way for all the multiform
Creations of their sons. Then let their sons
    Be not too proud that they have power to bind
New forces, but revere the daring ones
    Whose primal genius woke the human mind;
For none, however long the world may last,
Shall match those great inventors of the past.

¶ Heredity

The primitive Pithecanthropus erectus
With whom the ethnologists rightly connect us
   Defended his own
   By cudgel and stone;
Why isn't our ancestor here to protect us?

The arrogant Pithecanthropus erectus
Whose traits, through inheritance, deeply affect us,
   Was sure it was good
   To grab all he could,
Like some of his offspring whose morals deject us.

The ape man, the Pithecanthropus erectus,
Has many descendants prepared to dissect us;
   With them might is right,
   And if we can't fight
There's nothing at all that will make them respect us.

¶ Appeaser's Hymn
(*August 24, 1941*)

Onward, cautious soldiers,
    Marching short of war,
While the hordes of Hitler
    Wallow deep in gore!
When they bomb a neutral
    Thankfully we say,
"While so busy conquering
    They can't turn this way."
Onward, prudent soldiers
    Always short of war,
While the gang of Hitler
    Murders millions more!

The Pitcher that went to the well
   Is broken at last;
Disaster has sounded its knell.
   Its glory is past.

The Pitcher, undamaged and whole,
   That stayed on the shelf
And nursed a contemplative soul,
   Is pleased with itself.

"We mourn the unfortunate loss,"
   It placidly sighs,
"But rolling stones gather no moss
   And prudence is wise.

"Aloof from the turbulent race,
   Its bustle and noise,
A Pitcher should stay in its place
   And cultivate poise."

Nay, Pitchers of every make
    That skill can produce,
Since Pitchers, all Pitchers, must break,
    Be shattered in use.

For, good is the stress and the strife
    When Pitchers are brave,
And going to wells is the life
    A Pitcher should crave.

Before to destruction it fell,
    Again and again
The Pitcher that went to the well
    Gave water to men.

¶ The Law

"What doth the Lord require of thee but to do justly,
and to love mercy, and to walk humbly with thy God?"

The petty tyrants flout the truth,
    With force and fraud their deeds are done;
They grind the weak, they show no ruth.
    The great are just to every one.

The petty tyrants proudly go
    And where they march leave wreck behind;
They have no care for human woe.
    The great are merciful and kind.

The petty tyrants shout their claims
    That all shall tremble when they nod;
They bid men hail their noble names.
    The great walk humbly with their God.

The petty tyrants boast their power,
    But all the might they deem secure
Shall crash to earth with wall and tower.
    The great build strongholds that endure.

❡ To Commodore Matthew Calbraith Perry
(January, 1938)

When Commodore Perry with banners unfurled
Unbottled Japan on a wondering world,
How little he dreamed what a demon of war
Emerged from that bottle so harmless before —
A demon remorseless to ravage and kill,
Obeying no law but its arrogant will.
Oh, Commodore Perry, come quickly and pen
That spirit of wrath in its bottle again!

❡ The Eagle
(May 9, 1941)

The powers of evil arm for evil ends;
  With iron, food and oil in ample share
We give them aid, for what? To kill our friends
  And then ourselves. Greed-blinded fools, beware!

The soaring eagle whom the archer slew,
  When deeply stricken felt a double smart,
For, as the arrow pierced his breast, he knew
  That his own feathers winged the fatal dart.

ꝗ *A Scrap of Paper*

This document we sign with zeal
   And every pledge requirable,
Because the terms therein, we feel,
   For us are most desirable.

And this agreement, come what may,
   To every clause obedient,
We'll keep forever and a day
   As long as it's expedient.

ꝗ *A White Paper*

The Nazis are a gentle race;
They'd never kick you in the face,
But treat you like your dear old dad
If other people were not bad.
Because those others plan the worst,
The Nazis always do it first,
Yet bomb you as a parent would
And rule you solely for your good,
Say all, especially, of course,
The Czechs, the Poles, the Danes, the Norse.

¶ The Freedom of the Seize

(December 5, 1939)

We hardly had a navy when our history began,
We merely had a passion for the common rights of
man.
Our ships had oaken sheathing, but their crews were
bluff and hale,
And who was there to tell them where they might or
mightn't sail!
For when the Constitution flung her banner to the
breeze
Her cannon spoke in thunder for the freedom of the
seas.

Though now we have a navy that is sheathed in
heavy steel
And strong is every battleship from fighting-top to
keel,
The warring nations tell us, while we tremble in our
shoes,
What cargoes we may carry and what waters we
may cruise,

While meekly we oblige them, for we only strive to
    please,
Establishing their doctrine of the freedom of the
    seize.

9 Fashions for Fascists

Where tyranny's a passion
    And liberty is treason,
One color keeps in fashion
    For shirts through every season;

Since brown shirts hide their mud-stains,
    And red shirts dim the meaning
Of all their crimson blood-stains,
    While black shirts need no cleaning.

But shirts of freer nations
    Betray those blots and sploshings
That cause investigations
    And frequent public washings.

¶ Diplomatic Correspondence
(November 24, 1939)

"Dear Little Countries: Are you scared of ME?
And if so, please explain. R. S. V. P."

"Dear Fuehrer: *We're* not scared! — Don't look this
way so!
If we *were* scared, we'd be too scared to say so."

Forever honor those who, great of heart,
   Reared up the land we love and made it strong!
God give us equal strength to do our part
   As they did theirs, like them to face all wrong
Unflinchingly. As they were brave and just,
   So may we prove; and yet, as time in flight
Brings other ways, and better ways we trust,
   May we find nobler means to aid the right
Than their day knew. God's road is all uphill,
   And man climbs slowly. These were fine and true,
But we must bear their banner higher still;
   What else would those we honor have us do?
The past's a scroll whereon great truths are found,
But not a chain by which men's feet are bound.

You talk of miracles? René, my friend,
Let Father Paul explain their aim and end,
For miracles are not a soldier's trade;
Yet I can tell how miracles are made,
Because I made one. Yes, old comrade, I,
Robert de Baudricourt! Let none deny
This miracle of mine, though some would say
My part was but to speed it on its way.
Judge for yourself:

            You know how France was down;
We had a Dauphin whom we dared not crown,
A ruined country under half a king,
No courage, counsel, hope, nor anything,
The English armies, the Burgundian bands
Holding our castles, ravaging our lands,
We, helpless.

           Now, as simple as could be,
There came this village girl of Domremy
Demanding arms, protection of what sort
Lay in my power, with letters to the court.
And why? Why, God had sent her — God, no less —
Through voices, visions, saints, as you might guess,

To crown the Dauphin, put his foes to rout,
Save Orléans and drive the English out!
I sent her home.

                    But soon she came again.
The townfolk worshiped her; my trusted men
Believed in her and spoke for her; our plight
Was desperate; what else was there in sight?
I reasoned, "If she nerves these dull clods here
With zeal to snatch up battle-axe and spear
For France, she might move nobler sluggards, too."
And so I spoke with her as one might do
With some young squire — a handsome girl, as bright,
Direct and honest as the morning light.
I gossiped of the Dauphin, how he looked,
Held his head this way, kept two fingers crooked.
If she forgot such hints, as well she might,
Her saints would help her know her Prince at sight.
Some talk we had of war, which, you infer,
I meant her voices should recall to her
When steel was out. Then, with a sigh for France,
I gave her horse and helmet, sword and lance,
With some few men to guard her on her way
To Chinon, saying, "Go — let come what may."

What came, you know, the world knows.

Thus, you see,

I planned a miracle that came to be.

But she — that clear-eyed girl, the living flame
That swept the realm, that purged it of its shame,
Roused up the very dregs to strike and ward
And made the craven clamor for the sword —
Was she whose name is still a battle cry,
Who gave her land a soul that will not die,
Was she in truth a miracle divine,
I, but a paltry tool in God's design?

May Heaven send this world of blinded men
And cruelty that miracle again!

¶ Honor

(*May 22, 1941*)

"For you, the French people, it is simply a question of
following me without mental reservation along the
path of honor and national interest."
— MARSHAL PETAIN

What's honor? Human nature's saving grace —
Of doubtful worth in any market place,
A flame that lights few lamps, that boils no pot,
Yet drives imprudent souls, themselves forgot,
To hold it pure although all else be lost
And keep true faith no matter what the cost.
One can't eat honor, men may live without it,
But when 'tis gone, oh, never brag about it!

¶ Scene in Hell

Said Benedict Arnold to Judas, "Old pal,
Move over for Quisling and Monsieur Laval!"

¶ Neutrality

Republic, Principality,
Or Kingdom, shun Neutrality,
   That status of the milk-and-water blend!
The wielders of appliances
For murder make alliances;
   A neutral never keeps a single friend.

According to war's usances,
All pacifists are nuisances
   Whom combatants may bomb, or gas, or drown.
If meekness be your credo, you
May trust them to torpedo you,
   And you will have to take it lying down.

For War has proved legality;
But as for scared Neutrality,
   It cannot claim a solitary right.
Then, showing due civilities
To wagers of hostilities,
   Convince them that you're not too proud to fight.

❡ To C. I. O. and A. F. L.

Throw down your tools and wrangle, draw your
      fires,
  Harm industry and government alike,
"Strike — till the last armed foe expires;"
  What foe expires because you're out on strike?

❡ U. S. A.
(October 27, 1940)

Fair is the land from sea to sea,
Strong are its folk and bravely free;
Deaf if they are to a distant drum,
All will be true when the need shall come.

Tame though it seem when your war-cries cease,
Calm as the cote of the dove of peace,
Tyranny learn, if you can or will,
This is the eagle's aerie still!

¶ *"We've Got It to Do!"*

The river ran wild and the cataract roared;
We launched from the carry, our duffel aboard;
Our craft was a leaf for the torrent to fling,
And I a dead weight with an arm in a sling.
The guide in the stern with his paddle and pole
Was swinging the bow toward a point as a goal;
I said to him, "Dan, can you worry her through?"
He quietly answered, "I got it to do."

The trail may be doubtful or lost in a fog,
The road may be cumbered with windfall and bog,
The pack may be heavy, the pack may be strained
And high on the mountain the camp to be gained;
The sun may be hot or the wind may be chill,
A man may be weary or crippled or ill;
There may be a storm and a leaky canoe,
But who weighs the odds when we've got it to do?

The spirit that glowed in our old pioneers,
Our woodsmen and plainsmen, flames on through
    the years;

The spirit that tells us, though nothing be said,
To think and plan clearly, then drive straight ahead.
No sighing, no grumbling, no thought of despair,
But patient endurance and courage are there;
Whatever the toil on the path we must hew,
We'll finish our job when we've got it to do.

ꙡ Green Mountain Graveyard

All strife and enmity forgot,
   Beneath their native marble rest
The Tory and the Patriot,
   Their mother holds them to her breast.

Their mother who will not forget
   While grass grows green and river runs,
Still sings to these who paid their debt
   To warring causes, "Peace, my sons."

Their equal faith let all who bring
   Remembrance hither understand,
For this was loyal to his king,
   While that was loyal to his land.

¶ Ironmaster

Nathanael Greene left his forge
To fight the armies of King George,
Left his workmen at their labors
Beating plowshares into sabers,
Molding anchors into form
To hold the ship against the storm.
Tall and handsome, calm and steady,
Careful, watchful, ever ready,
General Greene with a soldier's pride
Drilled the lads of the countryside.
Best of all in the Cambridge tents
Were his trained Rhode Island regiments.

Nathanael Greene in woe and weal,
Arm of iron, soul of steel,
Proved his native metal's worth
Through the years of loss and dearth,
Formed anew the shattered line,
Stemmed the rout at Brandywine,
Cleared the Jerseys, held the right
Staunch and true at Monmouth fight.

When the beaten Southern forces
Fled from Camden, men and horses,
Greene, as Washington's right hand,
Brave and cautious, took command.
Greene the Yankee ironmaster
Saved the remnant from disaster;
General Greene in his threadbare cape
Hammered an army into shape,
Wrought again its iron core
On the flaming forge of War,
Fit for every chance alike,
Strong to bear and keen to strike.

Unafraid to face defeat,
Dangerous in planned retreat,
Quick to turn and deal a blow,
Wearing down a stronger foe,
Greene the blacksmith's hardy band
Led Cornwallis through the land
Over rivers, through morasses,
Tangled woods and rugged passes
North to Yorktown, where the trap
Closed upon him with a snap.

So the Noble Earl was caught
In the toils the blacksmith wrought.
Others linked the chain around him,
But who forged the steel that bound him,
Wringing triumph from disaster?
Greene the Yankee ironmaster!

9 *The Rocking Chair*

A Pilgrim Mother, being rather
More busy than the Pilgrim Father,
To many tasks at once attentive,
Became delightfully inventive
And made of apple-wood and leather
A cradle and a chair together
To rock as one upon three rockers;
Therein, despising ribald mockers,
She rocked, at one protracted sitting,
Her babe and self, and did her knitting.

The babe grew up; then, brokenhearted,
The cradle and the chair were parted;
That strange divorce — unprecedented
And many think to be lamented —
The antiquarians declare
Produced the well-known Rocking Chair.

This Rocking Chair and countless others
Gave comfort to the Pilgrim Mothers
But vexed and grieved the Pilgrim Sires;
Those farmers, traders, preachers, squires,

Returning late from Pilgrim sessions
Derived unfortunate impressions
Of Rocking Chairs; the rockers kicked them
In darkened rooms and tripped and nicked them,
Till, had it not been wrong to swear,
They would have cursed the Rocking Chair!

So Rocking Chairs might well have vanished
From Massachusetts, sternly banished
For stark irreverence or treason;
But one dark night in harvest season
Upon the hamlet undefended
The stealthy Indians descended!
With knives and tomahawks uplifted
Through well-swept vestibules they drifted
Ignoring scrapers, mats and knockers;
When, gallantly the ambushed rockers
Attacked the groping foe and floored him,
Their scythe-like cambers scratched and gored him,
They laid him low and saved from pillage
And savage rage the helpless village.

Since then the land's presumed possessors,
The Pilgrim Fathers' male successors

And remnants of the Knickerbockers,
Because those doughty chairs on rockers
Repulsed the copper-skinned invaders
And still discomfit midnight raiders,
Resign themselves to walk with care
And tolerate the Rocking Chair.

❡ The Answer

"Oh, Powers above that deign to rule
  Man's fortune, make me not a fool!"
    So prayed the fool with his last breath,
    Nor knew that he had prayed for death.

❡ Among the Angels

"Whence did you come?" The pilgrim answered,
    "Earth;
  A fevered planet, yet I loved it well."
Around him rang in soft, celestial mirth,
  "Why, that was Hell!"

¶ Vermont Marble

The shells of eons filled the deeps
Of ancient seas in mountain heaps
Of sifted lime that earthquake shock
And stress have crystallized to rock.

Now, cut and smoothed in pillared halls
It whitely gleams, or builds the walls
Of stately homes. Its remnant paves
Our village streets and marks our graves.

❡ Planting an English Oak
(World's Fair, 1939)

Small oak that grew with many an acorn peer
    From English earth upon the ancient tree
That harbored England's heir, be rooted here
    As English oaks in countries far and free
Are rooted.
                Like their oaks those nations stand,
    Those kindred realms of English speech and soul
That nurse no fear nor hate of any land
    Or race or creed, but strive to reach the goal
Of peace and justice.
              Little oak, grow strong
And flourish like your brothers; safe from blight,
From storm and thunderbolt and every wrong
    Of nature's violence or man's despite,
Lift starward, tower starward, bravely tall,
And may your boughs be broad to shelter all!

¶ Brave Laughter

Valor that laughs in the teeth of disaster,
Courage that makes Fate the friend, not the master,
These are of England, her kith and her kin;
Brave laughter shall win.

HOMO SAP

Where you find them worshiping an ass,
Call him beautiful and bring him grass.

It makes the prize dog's lot a great deal cheerier
To feel that other dogs are much inferior.

Brief Essay on Man

Aspiring Man, by learned pens
Once classed as Homo sapiens,
Is now, the poor, deluded chap,
Correctly labeled, Homo sap.

⁋ *Outline of Evolution*

The first amoeba, as the one and only
Existing animal, was sad and lonely;
He split himself in two amoeban pieces,
Preparing for the Origin of Species.

Their brats were foraminifers and corals;
Then polyzoans, quaint, though lacking morals,
And forms of life now used as toothsome dishes,
Like gastropods, lamellibranchs and fishes.

These throve and multiplied beneath the waters;
But their more enterprising sons and daughters,
Discarding gills and all aquatic trammels,
Emerged as insects, reptiles, birds and mammals.

From reptiles grew tremendous dinosauri,
Though huge, deficient in the upper story;
From these the mammals came, some way or other,
With Man, or *Homo Sapiens*, our brother.

This upstart, Man, once Nature's Lilliputian,
Esteems himself the Crown of Evolution;
But he will sink beneath Creation's mire
Unless he evolutes a whole lot higher.

ℊ Our Absurd Past

How funny people seem when we review
The eighteen-eighties and the nineties, too!
While some played poker, drank and bet on horses,
They looked askance on multiple divorces,
And though conflicting tendencies were tending,
Believed in saving rather than in spending.
They harbored strange ideas of entertainment;
Their lack of bridge deserves severe arraignment,
For friends could spend an evening merely talking;
They bicycled, they even stooped to walking!
The critics did not feel obliged to utter
Hurrahs for books in language of the gutter,
And though some liked burlesque shows gay and
    gaudy,
None ever praised a play for being "bawdy."
How quaint they were! How much our world has
    brightened
Since we're sophisticated and enlightened!

9 *The Chip on the Shoulder*

Learn this now before you are older:
Don't go through life with a chip on your shoulder,
Always aggrieved and ever offended,
Fancying wrongs that are not intended.
Let not a sense of humor desert you,
Take it that nobody means to hurt you,
Find no insult in idle chatter,
Pass it over; it doesn't matter.
Look for the best in everybody,
Value the wool, forget the shoddy;
Get in the habit of liking people.
Love is the spire on every steeple.

❡ Note for Legislators

Eels get used to being skinned,
Like sardines to being tinned.
Hens get used to being axed,
Men get used to being taxed.

❡ The Ides

The Soothsayer whispered from behind the arch
To Caesar, "Ssst! Beware the ides of March!"
But Caesar answered, laughing, "*Tecum pax!*
Beware yourself! I've paid *my* income tax!"

9 Fortune Telling

The psychic solves the darkest mystery
   By arts that none may understand;
The palmist reads your mortal history
   In lines engraved upon your hand;
The medium reveals our missions
Through interviews with apparitions.

Stargazers learn from high astrology
   Our fates while we pursue our slumbers,
While advocates of numerology
   Prove destiny controlled by numbers,
Including calculus, quadratics
And all the higher mathematics.

With packs of cards not used in poker
   The gypsies tell what's bound to be
(A Romany once drew a joker
   And turned the thing, face-up, at me!);
To skilled interpreters of tea leaves
Full many a simple soul a fee leaves.

On some whose skulls have unknit sutures
    Such fortune tellers ever prey,
But you can read your pasts and futures
    And choose your course as well as they;
Cry "heads" or "tails" and toss a penny,
You'll get as good results as any.

¶ What Are the Short Waves Saying?

Hark to the broadcast of news!
　Maybes, perhaps and mights,
Buts, propaganda and views,
　Experts' rhetorical flights.

Hints that a censor ignores,
　Facts and perversions of facts,
Wars and the rumors of wars,
　Pacts and the rumors of pacts.

¶ Real-Estate Business

Our city's rich in thoroughfares with charming
    designations
Appropriate in meaning for all tastes and occupations.

We offer homes and offices and stores to show your
    wares
On proper streets and avenues or places, parks, and
    squares.

For clergymen, could anything be pleasanter to hear
Than Rector, Vestry, Church, and Dean, and
    possibly Revere?

There's peace in Haven Avenue, returning from a
    journey,
And lawyers take to Chambers Street, or better still,
    Attorney.

Some artists favor Carmine Street, while others seek
    renown
In Black or White, Green Avenue, or else the Place
    called Brown.

Should Little Street appear too small, it only costs a
    nickel
To go to Longstreet Avenue, or, if you're Scotch, to
    Mickle.

One applicant, a jeweler, we've furnished with a list
That features Gold and Silver Streets with Pearl and
    Amethyst.

An electrician whom we serve has lately changed his
    home;
He dwelt on Ampere Avenue, but now he lives on
    Ohm.

Another client, strange to tell, prefers to use his feet;
From Carr, then Rider Avenue, he's moved to
    Walker Street.

To tempt bird lovers, "Audubon" is all we need to
    say,
Appending Starling, Vireo, and maybe Drake and
    Jay,

While Buck and Fox and Beaver, Hunter Avenue
and Fowler,
With Forest, Camp, and Falconer Streets allure the
wildwood prowler.

Of Taylor, Glover, Baker, certain trades are rightly
fond,
And financiers and brokers like the sound of Bank
and Bond.

But should you scorn these offers and repel them
with disdain,
We've nothing left but Sexton Place and Cemetery
Lane.

9 Names and Numbers

Though fog or night the scene encumbers,
Why don't all buildings show their numbers
   On lintel, wall or door?
Why can't a house say good and plenty,
"Hey, look at me! I'm Nineteen-twenty,
   The joint you're looking for!"

Why can't our thoroughfares, our highways,
Our squares, our streets, our parks, our byways,
   Have signs where all can see?
"I'm Lincoln Place." "I'm Pershing Corner."
"I'm Avenue Ignatius-Horner."
   "I'm Boulevard Legree."

But what appears the very oddest
Is that our towns are all so modest
   And loath to urge their claims.
Why not proclaim whenas we enter
"Podunk, the World's Great Peanut Center?"
   Why don't they tell their names?

So, dwellings, mansions, roadways, alleys,
As well as rivers, mountains, valleys,
    And hamlets near and far
Throughout this self-effacing nation,
We really want the information;
    Please tell us who you are!

Ꝙ Farewell to the Aquarium

Displaced by a tunnel,
A submarine funnel
From Brooklyn to Battery Park,
"Good-by!" our sea lions,
Those musical scions
Of ocean reproachfully bark.
Good-by and best wishes
To all the sweet fishes,
The turtles so calm and sedate,
The gay sons and daughters
Of tropical waters
As well as the carp and the skate!
The sinuous conger
May charm us no longer;
Good-by to the rainbow-hued wrasse!
The grunts, the crustaceans
And all their relations
Who goggled and gaped through the glass!
No habeas corpus
Could save us a porpoise,

A sea horse, a fluke or a ray.
Commissioner Moses
Who opens and closes
Has moved our fish circus away!

9 At La Guardia Field

I would not be the prideful plane
    Bazooming as it flies
Above the rugged mountain chain,
    Across the starry skies.

I'd rather be the little truck
    That on the parking space
Will grab that airplane by the tail
    And put it in its place.

9 *A Fable for Litigants*

Two Porpoises, colliding in the smother
Of stormy seas, grew angry with each other,
And, claiming damages, as some will do
For injured dignity, resolved to sue.
So each of them engaged a Legal Shark
To plead his cause. But, meeting after dark,
Those Legal Sharks discussed their private ends,
Agreeing wisely, "Let us still be friends;
We must not let our clients' grudges warp us;
Besides, there's nothing fatter than a Porpoise,
And what with fees, and costs, and habeas corpuses
We both may profit while we're at Cross Porpoises."

¶ Wedding Gift Alphabet
(Acknowledgments by an Ungrateful Bride)

A is Aunt Alice who sent the Armchair;
We wish it would let us forget it was there.

B is for Bosworth who gave us the Books
Too dreary to read but the binding's de luxe.

C is for Clifford who mailed us a Check
So big we could fall on the dear fellow's neck.

D is for Delia who sent us the Desk
Too fragile to write on, but so picturesque!

E is for Elmer who sent us the Ewer;
We wish that our presents of that sort were fewer.

F is for Felix who sent us the Fork
He got as a souvenir once in New York.

G's Cousin Gertrude who sent us the Globe
Which must be on show when she comes from
      Latrobe.

H is for Hetty who sent us the Honey,
Quite good, but I think for a wedding it's funny.

I is for Ida who sent the Ice-Pitcher
Which wouldn't be bad if the chasing were richer.

J is for various things from Japan
That we must get rid of as fast as we can.

K is for Kenneth who sent us the Knives;
I fear they will haunt us the rest of our lives.

L is for Leonard who shipped us the Lamp;
We've seven or eight of a similar stamp.

M is for Minnie who sent us the Mat
With "Welcome" upon it — She isn't, the cat!

N is for Nelson who sent us the Nest
Of tables, for bridge he intends to suggest.

O is for Olive; the glass Olive-dish
She sent us is all that an olive could wish.

P is for Peter who sent us the Platter,
A little bit tarnished, but that doesn't matter.

Q is for Quintus who gave us a Quart
Of excellent whiskey, for moral support.

R is for Raymond who shipped us the Rug;
It's grand, so I'll send him a kiss and a hug.

S is for Stanwood who sent us the Spoons
That probably cost him a dozen doubloons.

T is Theresa who sent the Tureen
That cannot be used but is meant to be seen.

U is Umberto who sent us the Urn,
And how we can lose it I'm dying to learn.

V is Viola who sent us the Vase
That's marked for an accident one of these days.

W's Worthington's gift, the What-is-it;
He'll tell what it's for when he pays us a visit.

X is for Xavier who slipped us twelve X's,
Our favorite cousin of either two sexes.

Y's Uncle Yarrow who sent us his Yacht —
The model, of course, but we like it a lot.

Z's Uncle Zeno whose present is Zero;
When I write my novel he won't be the hero!

⁊ Aquarium Note

People keep guppies
To watch them have puppies;
This practice, quite recent
And not wholly decent,
Shows how modernity
Honors maternity.

¶ Sunday School Story

A boy there was who, day and night, until he grew
    too old to,
Went off to school and up to bed the instant he was
    told to.

In later years he ran a race, and when he met his
    master,
Declared the other fellow won by going so much
    faster.

When grown, he did his work with zeal and skill
    unprecedented
And met his notes and paid his bills the day they
    were presented.

And he became a statesman, who, to everybody's
    wonder,
Outspokenly admitted that just once he'd made a
    blunder!

❦ Motto for a Beauty Parlor

No beauty gives delight to every eye,
Except your beauty, dear; and who knows why
The Hippopota-miss, grotesque to us,
Looks lovely to her Hippopotamus?

❦ Excelsior!

Now why do social climbers climb
To frigid heights and waste their time
When all they meet, poor masking mimers,
Upon the top are other climbers
Regarding them with looks severe
That ask, "And how did *you* get here?"

9 Grandeur

The City Mouse dropped from a westbound diner;
He sniffed, "Though the air may be somewhat finer
Than back in the East, the effects are cruder
And everything's notably rougher, ruder —"
When he was surprised by a slap of the tail from
A Country Mouse with a "Whar d'you hail from?"

The City Mouse, lifting an eyebrow slightly,
Responded austerely and yet politely
While nibbling a casual bit of cereal,
"I dwell in the Grand Hotel Imperial,
The final word in comfort blended
With all that is sumptuous, rich and splendid.
We've a thousand rooms with bathing facilities,
Indirect lighting and such utilities;
And all of the other permanent residents
Are princes, generals, dukes and presidents.
And, since I see only a railway station,
Might one inquire your habitation?"

"I live," said the other, with some bravado,
"In this great Grand Canyon of the Colorado

Which runs, my cultured Eastern friend,
Two hundred miles from end to end.
It's one mile deep and twelve miles wide
And we could lose your town inside.
You can't find anywhere, by gracious,
A home more sumptuous, rich and spacious.
Why, kings and queens from the farthest nations
Come here to look at the decorations!"
Said the Country Mouse with a gay gambado,
"Meet the Grand Canyon of the Colorado!"

9 You and Your Conscience

First, Conscience gives your soul a sting
And after that keeps whispering,
"Oh, you were bad! — And what about
Explaining when you get found out?"
That painful thought disturbs your rest,
Because you wonder, "Is it best
To own that I was wrong or lax,
Or could I cover up my tracks?"
While Conscience gossips with Remorse,
You take the customary course
Of finding every means of hiding
Your bit of indiscreet backsliding.
When this is done, released from care,
You turn and jeer at Conscience, "There!
That wasn't any harm at all!"
And Conscience, feeling mighty small,
Impertinent and ill at ease,
Contritely begs, "Excuse it, please!"

The skeleton is hiding in the closet as it should,
The needle's in the haystack and the trees are in the
      wood,
The fly is in the ointment and the froth is on the beer,
The bee is in the bonnet and the flea is in the ear.

The meat is in the coconut, the cat is in the bag,
The dog is in the manger and the goat is on the crag,
The worm is in the apple and the clam is on the shore,
The birds are in the bushes and the wolf is at the door.

These people shall be barred by stern command
From that fair realm, the children's perfect land:
People who promise, but don't keep their promises,
And thus make children grow up Doubting
    Thomases;
People who don't know any better than
To bleat, "My, my! You're quite a little man!"
People who ask whose little lady this is,
Or will insist that children give them kisses;
People with shaky nerves or bad digestions
Who snap when children ask important questions;
People who can't forget, but scold them so
For something children did a week ago;
People who stare and stare, while children tremble,
Deciding which relation they resemble;
People who won't let children make a noise;
People who play with children's chosen toys;
People who can't be natural, but giggle
And chatter baby talk while children wriggle;
And in the children's land there shan't and won't
Be people who are always saying, "Don't!"

¶ *Sincere Sympathy*

With words of consolation we would tenderly express
Our grief for all who suffer or who fail to win success,
For boys who have no motor cars, for Kings who
have no thrones,
For girls who have no permanents and dogs who have
no bones.

Impartially we're sorry for the kitten and the mouse,
As sorry for the Senate as we're sorry for the House,
And sorry for the President, unsleepingly on guard,
As well as for the Nation that he rules so awful hard.

We're sorry for all persons who receive or need relief,
We're sorry for the victim, yet we're sorry for the
thief,
And sorry for the jurors who are rounded up in
twelves,
But sorriest for people who are sorry for themselves!

⁊ Retribution

Yes, Joe is dead, mah good-fer-nothin' Joe.
You t'ought he wuz a worker? Lawzy! No,
He'd never do a thing but sit an' sit —
Him help me? Bless you, Missy, not a bit!
But now I got him fixed, an' fixed fer fair;
I had dat man cremated! Yes. An' dere
You see his ashes in dat hour glass
Whut I keeps turnin' while de work-hours pass,
An' so dat man whut loafed his life away,
Keeps runnin', runnin', runnin' all de day!

¶ Subject to Change Without Notice

Little Off'n-Onnie has said she'll come today,
Which means she could, perhaps she won't, and yet
    again she may.
You rarely know when she might go, and never
    when she'll come,
For, oscillating to and fro, her will's a pendulum.

Whatever she declares she'll do, her promise more
    or less
Will shift its weight to yes and no and then to no
    and yes.
This fact alone about her plans you may depend
    upon,
That nothing makes it wholly sure that they are off
    or on.

While if and as and when she comes she'll bring a
    toilet case
Equipped with stuff and implements for making up
    the face,
She really needs a special one exclusively designed
With stabilizing fixatives for making up the mind.

¶ Reprieved

"My brother," Rhadamanthus said
  To Minos, "when we judge the dead,
  Why not lay bare to every one
  The deeds of darkness each has done?"
  Said Minos, "While this might be well
  For hardened miscreants of Hell,
  I gather from their record rolls
  That even our exalted souls
  Would writhe, exposed when disembodied,
  Poor sinners!" Rhadamanthus nodded.
"And so perhaps we'd best resign us
  To call the whole thing off?" said Minos.
  Then, lightly waving an acanthus,
  "We'll call it off," said Rhadamanthus.

❡ The Army Mule

The mule
Is no man's fool;
Reserved and cool,
He tugs not till he's heard
The properly improper word.
A connoisseur of cursory remarks,
He stirs not till the teamster barks
The picturesque profanity
Of vigorous humanity.
The dialect may be of any nation,
But if it's rich in fervent objurgation,
With ears spread wide
He marks in joy and pride
His driver's eloquence
And moves from hence to thence.

Persuade the ass
With thistles, hay, or grass;
Subject the horse
By means of oats or force

Beneath your rule!
The free-born mule
Will only do as you desire him
When red hot epithets inspire him,
But, whether shrilled in tenor or falsetto,
The music moves him more than the libretto.

⁊ Outdoor Furniture

Banish cold marble benches from your garden!
The longer sat upon, the more they harden,
While fancy iron seats, still more uncanny,
Impress quaint patterns on the human fanny.
But lounging chairs, the kind they use on steamers,
Upon your lawn give peace to idle dreamers.

ℊ Contentment

When spring arrives and lilacs blow
I'm not compelled to shovel snow.
In summer no one bothers me
To feed a fire, nor skate, nor ski.
In autumn one no longer needs
To waste the morning pulling weeds.
And winter brings no dewy dawn
When I must rise to mow the lawn.

So I am glad the seasons through
For what I do not have to do.

¶ Suggesting a Compromise

The eagle's joy is flying where he will,
The clam is happy simply lying still.
The eagle rends his prey and rears his brood,
The ocean serves the clam his daily food.
Oh, would you rather be the splendid, regal,
Ambitious, fighting, ever-soaring eagle,
Or would you be the calm and blissful clam
Who eats and sleeps and doesn't give a damn —
Or else, contented yet not wholly selfish,
A cross between the eagle and the shellfish?

¶ Weather Report

No one could ever imagine how horrid a
Ch-ch-ch-chill we are having in Florida!
North winds are raging, the rose petals scattering,
Fingers are frozen and teeth are ch-chattering,
Shoulders are shaky, sh-shuddery, shivery,
Oil stoves and hearth wood are cash on delivery.
Only our sea birds, those simply incurable
Optimists, find the conditions endurable.
Skirting the camp where the trailers are mustering,
Down where the tourists forlornly are clustering
Close to their litter of papers and smelly cans,
Sail the armadas of mallards and pelicans
Passing the signs reading "Esso" and "Texaco,"
Breasting the waves of the blue Gulf of Mexico.
Little they bother, although I am told it is
Well under freezing, how bitterly cold it is,
Warm in their covering, plumy and leathery.
W-w-w-would that my clothing were feathery!

9 The Imp of Forgetfulness

A Demon called Putah, the Prince of Forgetting,
Has wiles that to Man are completely upsetting.
He touches the brow with his devilish ointments,
And who can remember his dates and appointments!

However you boast of your mental resources,
Mnemonic devices and memory courses,
Whenever that basely insidious plotter
Applies to the brain his oblivious blotter,

The string on the finger, the scribblings on paper,
The knot in the handkerchief vanish like vapor.
That number, that name, that exact information
He carries away as his favorite ration.

Old Satan himself couldn't manage to beat him.
But, wait! I remember a way to defeat him!
Or, rather, I did; but, I deeply regret it,
That scandalous Putah has made me forget it!

¶ The King's English

Beware, Our Sovereign Lord of Britain!
Preserve our English, whether written
Or spoken, from the fatal tang
Of this atrocious Yankee slang!

Suppose His Grace of Canterbury
Should sigh, "Your majesty, that's very
Improper; for, what says Isaiah"—
And you should interrupt, "Oh ye-ah?"

Suppose your most important minister
Should groan, "The situation's sinister;
We're bound to act, beyond a doubt."
And you should say, "Include me out!"

Suppose, behind the royal curtain,
Your Council should insist, "It's certain
That this is what we'll have to do."
And you should answer back, "Sez you!"

Your Majesty, our tongue's protection,
Avoid American infection
And let us keep the speech we've got
In all its purity! Eh, wot?

⁊ Poem for Purists

"A preposition is a bad word to end a sentence with."

I see a storm careering through the notch, from
My window seat — a cozy place to watch from.

A vapor sweeps before in swirling shreds, up
The valley, but the maples keep their heads up.

Now rain descends and makes a tempting pool by
The pathway that the children go to school by,

And trickles through a leak that should be seen to
By someone — yes, I know it, and I mean to!

Reverberating detonations crash in
The cumuli that lightnings also flash in,

A turbid torrent overflows the brink of
The winding river that our cattle drink of,

The ripening butternuts come thumping down on
The pavement that the fallen leaves are brown on,

While I am praying that I won't offend with
These prepositions that I love to end with!

𝓰 Victorian Relapse

That isn't Henry the Eighth as you feared,
Christopher Morley is growing a beard,
Decking his chin with the silkiest fuzz;
Come and admire it, everyone does,
Calling it sweet with a touch of the weird;
Christopher Morley is growing a beard.
Publishers, poets and tellers of tales
View this adornment peculiar to males,
Anxiously whispering, "Shall it be sheared?"
Christopher Morley is growing a beard.

9 *What Every Publisher Knows*

All writers
Are blighters.
They persuade you to print their stuff
Though it's far from good enough,
And then to waste in advertising
Sums that are astounding and surprising.
They think that books are plastic
And forms of type elastic,
For, sitting proudly aloof,
They scribble new chapters in proof
That should have been in their original copy —
A practice deplorably sloppy
That doesn't make sense
And entails trouble and expense.
Strangely thinking you capable of misleading them,
They won't sign contracts without reading them,
And when they do, they insist on mercenary
    alterations
That disturb harmonious relations,
And evidence a greed
Which, in authors, is shocking indeed.

What is most distressful,
If you make their books successful,
Instead of sticking to you with decent loyalty,
They change to a competitor who offers a bigger
    royalty!

They are biters
Of the hand that feeds them, these ungrateful writers!

ADAM TO EVE

I am loved by the moon! Then why should I care
What the stars may think as they twinkle there?

To him who steals my heart's delight,
A toothache and a long, long night!

⁊ Adam to Eve

What ages passed before a fragment torn
   From chaos whirled through unimagined spaces!
What ages more beheld this planet born
   And slowly filled with dull and brutish races!

To think, while dragons rose from froth and scum
   And strove for mastery with might unequal,
How many dreadful chances might have come
   To bar or change the perfect, golden sequel!

I trembled with remembered hopes and fears
   Among gross monsters, bellowing and snarling,
Until, the flower of those uncounted years,
      Came you, my darling!

¶ Serenade

Delicious, delectable, dainty, delightful,
　　Adorable, darling and dear,
All words that caress you and praise you are rightful,
　　So come to your window and hear,
　　　　My dear!

Enchanting, entrancing, alluring, enthralling,
　　Enrapturing, winsome and sweet,
Oh, turn not away when your lover is calling
　　And laying his heart at your feet,
　　　　My sweet!

Appear like the moon that above you is riding
　　In loveliness less than your own,
Shine out like a star that a mist has been hiding
　　On him who adores you alone,
　　　　My own!

9 The Trail

The trail you made is somewhere beaten plain,
　　And elsewhere faintly marked in vale and hollow;
But through the wood, across the mountain chain,
　　　　Your trail I follow.

That ever-upward path I often lose
　　Where undergrowth and fallen timbers blind it;
But though I pause in doubt which way to choose,
　　　　I always find it.

I may not reach your camp; my strength may fail
　　Among the clouds that gather dark and sodden;
I only know that I must keep the trail
　　　　Your feet have trodden.

❡ *The Cabin*

What is this fragrant home of ours
Beneath the Pine that starward towers?

"A place with nooks wherein to nest,"
Flutes robin of the ruddy breast.

"A place," the saucy squirrels hold,
"Of snug retreat from winter's cold."

"A mystery whereat to peer
And bound away from!" snorts the deer.

To our returning hearts it seems
A port for caravels of dreams,

A magic bourne of calm release
Where burdens fall and troubles cease,

A shrine below a mountain spur,
A sanctuary built of fir

With door flung wide to wind and sun,
And, when the happy day is done,

A casket stored with love and light
Enwrapped in velvet vasts of night.

¶ Lightness

Light are the things I love the best;
Light as a cloud on the mountain crest,
Light as a puff of thistledown,
Light as the bluebell's dancing gown,
Light as a poising humming-bird,
Light as the chime of a lovely word,
Light as the foam of a waterfall,
Light as a dream beyond recall,
Light as the veil of rising mist,
Light as the evening amethyst,
Light as the fur on a willow slip,
Light as the touch of a baby's lip,
Light as the gloss on a barley straw,
Light as the pat of a kitten's paw,
Light as the thread that spiders spin,
Light as the tread of a moccasin,
Light as the rosebud's drop of dew,
Light as the lift of a birch canoe,
Light as a heart that's free of care,
Light as a tress of waving hair,
Light as the song the wood thrush sings —
   Why must I love light things?

꧋ Relic

This golden-brown Cremona violin
   From which the bow of Paganini drew
Pure magic — now forever hushed within
   A crystal shrine for reverent eyes to view,
Would rather be the nameless instrument
   That, gayly timed by children's dancing feet,
Goes singing to the end, improvident,
   Played by the laughing gypsy in the street.

9 *Are You a Man or a Mouse?*

The friendly angel, Raphael,
   Flew down where Paradise lay sleeping,
And there beside a crystal well
   Was Eve, disconsolately weeping.

The seraph smiled, "Why do you grieve?"
   And while his golden aura brightened
The leafy grove, "Poor me!" sobbed Eve,
   "So timid, helpless, weak and frightened!

"I'm dreadfully afraid of mice,
   And snakes that beam and call me 'Madam,'
And bats and bugs; and once or twice
   I've even been afraid of Adam!"

"Fair mother of the human clan,"
   Said Raphael, "your daughters' dower
And yours shall be this talisman —
   The consciousness of secret power.

"Although alarmed at little things,
    Flood, fire and steel shall not dismay you,
Whose feet shall tread the necks of kings
    While men adoringly obey you.

"Hold high that lovely head! Until
    The world-consuming embers crackle,
Shall Adam bend before you still,
    Your place his shrine, his tabernacle."

So, even as in Paradise,
    We bow us in that House of Rimmon.
If women are afraid of mice,
    Mere men are more afraid of women.

❧ Compensation

What future guerdon shall amend the pain
Of those that here have loved, but loved in vain?
Ask not; for these who missed, as fate befell,
Their hearts' desire were blessed in loving well.
But pray that some atoning grace may fall
On those poor souls that never loved at all.

❧ Morning Song

Dear little head on the pillow,
   Eyes with the light of a star,
Throat like the foam of the billow,
   How precious you are!

Loveliness ever beside me,
   Smiles that are answering mine,
These, though all else be denied me,
   Make life divine.

9 The Steel Wedding

The toast of all the Eastern Shore,
    As Maryland's divinest daughter,
Was lovely Ann, and by the score
    The richest and the proudest sought her.

But Francis Bayard claimed her hand,
    And when from station, wealth, and glitter
She turned to him at Love's command,
    Oh, many hearts grew dark and bitter!

And when she walked, a winsome bride,
    To chapel, blessed by kindly viewers,
The aisle was thronged on either side
    By jealous maids and jilted wooers.

"If aught forbids that these may wed,"
    (Was that a hint of jeering laughter?)
"Declare it now," the parson read,
    "Or hold your peace forever after."

A murmur rose: "The jilt! The jade!"
 The parson paused and thumbed the psalter;
The bridegroom drew his sword and laid
 The threatening steel across the altar.

The murmur died. While all around
 Was hushed as woods in windless weather,
The parson spoke the words that bound
 A man and maid for life together.

And they were held the blithest pair
 'Twixt Chesapeake and Ocean's border,
For Ann was true as she was fair —
 And Francis kept his house in order.

꧁ Treasure-Trove

Pearls are hid within the shell,
   Gold is at the rainbow's ending,
Truth is down the deepest well,
   Song is with the lark ascending.

Truth and beauty, pearls and gold,
   Song, the loveliest and clearest —
All are mine to have and hold,
   For you are in my heart, my dearest!

9 The Unseen Lover

Never be lonely again, my treasure,
   Never be weary again, my own;
I shall be with you in grief and pleasure,
   Close to your soul as to yours alone.

That is the warmth of my arms about you,
   That is my kiss on your lips and brow;
Never again shall I yearn without you,
   Never in vain shall you call me now.

Long through the worlds in their cloudy smother,
   Deep in the vault of eternal blue,
Life after life we have sought each other,
   Asking of shadows, "Can this be you?"

Shadows were all till the veil was rifted,
   When, in the hour that was meant to be,
Came we transfigured, with arms uplifted,
   I to you, darling, and you to me.

Past is our questioning, when or whether;
   Nothing may hold us bereft, apart.
Ever as one we shall cleave together,
   Spirit to spirit and heart to heart.

❡ So Little

So little seem such lovely things,
　　The hummingbird, the twinkling star,
The butterfly on wayward wings,
　　Yet doubly dear they are.

And you, my little rose-in-bloom,
　　My little pearl that needs no art,
Take up so very little room,
　　But how you fill my heart!

❡ Lost, Strayed, or Stolen

Bureau of Missing Persons, where can my darling be?
Bureau of Missing Persons, who else so missed as she—
The daintiest, the fairest, of all from coast to coast?
And I'm the missing person that misses her the most.

How long since last I saw her? An endless hour ago.
And what's she like, you ask me? Take everything
    you know
Or dreamed about of beauty and loveliness, and then
Add all of it together and multiply by ten.

But what might be her danger? So many ills I fear—
I've dreaded lest the south wind might steal away my
    dear;
I've trembled lest the angels, the mermaids, or the
    elves
Might claim her as their kindred and take her to
    themselves.

But now I catch a fragrance like violets of May
And see a herald sunbeam that's like the peep of day

And mark a footfall, airy as thistledown on foam—
Bureau of Missing Persons, don't mind; she's coming
home!

❧ Flamingo Dance

A star peeps through where the twilight fades,
The moonlight falls on the Everglades;
Up on the grasslands' broad expanse
The proud flamingos dance their dance.

Come in pairs and form quadrilles,
   Leave your nestlings, take your places,
Arch your necks and click your bills,
   March with measured, stately paces!

Forward, backward, weave in rings
   While the owl is calling, calling;
Lift and wave your scarlet wings
   Where the flame vine blooms are falling!

When the ever-watchful moon
Hangs above the dark lagoon,
Some may see by happy chance
The proud flamingos dance their dance.

❡ *Meteor*

The fragment of a star, I hung in space
    Until as bathed in silver upward rolled
Your lovely Earth, she drew me from my place;
    I rushed to meet her through the breathless cold
Of emptiness; her warm caress of air
    Enkindled me; I blazed across her night,
A globe of splendor with a trailing flare
    Of burning gold, portentous to the sight
Of dazzled millions — till my fire was drowned
    In marl. With crash and roar I struck the field,
Driving my smoldering metal under ground
    To lie forgot, my secret unrevealed,
Again a ragged shard without a name;
    But, for one glorious moment, I was Flame!

CLEAN WATERS

That is hid which no one sees or hears,
But — the day has eyes, the night has ears.

Choose your neighbor, then your near abode;
Choose your comrade, first, and then your road.

9 *Clean Waters*

The waters of the world are Heaven's gift
  To all that live; let them be ever pure,
Pure as the snows that in the craggy rift
  Melt to renew those fountains that allure
The doe and fawn, pure as the mountain stream,
  The river where but woods and meadows are,
The fern-fringed lake — pure as the crystal's gleam,
  Pure as the dreamy radiance of a star.
Redeem from dark defilement every flow
  Befouled by greed and wastage; call a sea
As sapphire-clear as Ocean long ago
  To break on shores as unpolluted; free
Our waters of their shame, and they shall bless
The land again with health and wholesomeness.

¶ Dream Trout

Right through the center of our country town,
    Above the church and twenty yards below
The store, a runnel comes cascading down
    When we've had rain enough to prime its flow.
Beside this rill with net and rod and reel,
    In wading boots correctly fitted out,
A small boy stood, his wicker fishing creel
    All ready for imaginary trout.
Oh, never glimmered fish more bright to see
    Than these, believed in, though not really there.
As well he knows, yet miracles may be,
    And faith is joy enough. So may we share
With that small boy, to whom we're all akin,
    A doubtproof creel to keep our dream trout in.

¶ Hillborn

I

"We own the land," the plainsmen swear,
"We own the land we fence and till!"
The mountain men are silent, where
The land owns them, and always will.

II

Two ranges rim our valley
With scant a league between
The marble-ribbed Taconics,
The granite-crested Green.

Where here a torrent gushes,
And there a cataract gleams;
The marble and the granite
Are in those mountain streams.

We drink the living waters
That come through channeled stone;
Their marble and their granite
Are in our brawn and bone.

III

Warm Brook flows westward, calm and still,
   The Fayville like an avalanche
   To mingle in the Roaring Branch
That billows into Batten Kill.

And Batten Kill rolls on to join
   Old Hudson; threading vale and glen
   The waters keep their tryst, as when
They blocked the march of John Burgoyne.

The streams, the woods, the hills above
   This plot of earth that holds our dead
   Have battled for the men they bred
As men defend the land they love.

¶ Country Doctor

Old Doc Smith has his rounds to go
To the ill and well, to the high and low,
And he plows his way through the whirl of snow,
  The worst of the blizzard weather scorning.
Then it's "Out with your tongue, and let me see;
You have athlete's foot, you have housemaid's knee,
So you'll drink this down and you'll sleep," says he,
  "And you'll be all right in the morning."

Old Doc Smith, with his pills and such,
Is wise and shrewd with the human touch,
And he knows right off that you ate too much,
  So he shakes his finger for a warning.
Then he gives you a dose that is black and strong,
And its taste is bitter and it lasts too long,
But you're glad when he laughs — for he can't be
    wrong —
  "You'll be all right in the morning."

Old Doc Smith has a lot to do,
He has far to go and he's never through,
So you can't see how he has time for you
     With all the dying and a-borning.
But he'll put you to bed and he'll tuck you in,
And you know you'll live; for you see him grin
And you hear him growl as he strokes his chin,
     "You'll be all right in the morning."

¶ News from Vermont

Our Governor, George Aiken,
Who cannot be mistaken,
   Declares Vermont is feeling simply great
And neither glum nor chirpless
Because we have a surplus
   In this our most extraordinary State.

Our kitten, known as Myrtle,
That wears a coal black kirtle
   And at its throat the snowiest of flecks,
Was named, with taste unbeaten,
By Walter Prichard Eaton,
   While Mrs. Eaton diagnosed its sex.

Right after that was written
We got a second kitten,
   Much younger and of Persian pedigree,
Whose gender none can tell us;
But Myrtle's awful jealous
   And hisses like a critic on a spree.

We've heard from Maxwell Aley
And Tom Augustine Daly,
   And just have had a glimpse of Robert Frost!
The Canfields, Hards and Fishers
With all of his well-wishers
   Are glad he isn't stolen, strayed or lost.

That ancient cattle stable
Where dwelt the cow named Mabel
   Has been revised to house your motor car.
Though I've abjured the flagon
(In short, am on the wagon),
   I keep my noted skill in tending bar.

We fill for your vagaries
The cup that, as it varies,
   Inebriates perchance, or merely cheers;
But Mr. Sinclair Lewis
May claim a bowl of brewis
   Although we haven't met for thirty years.

We love our quiet labors,
Our visitors, our neighbors,
   Our mountains with the sunset in between;
And Alexander Woollcott
Shall have the little hall cot
   Whenever he comes down from Bomoseen.

⁊ The State Seal Pine

Three centuries the pine has stood
  Firm-rooted on its hill,
The last of all the ancient wood
  Above the Battenkill;

Three hundred crowding years and more,
  And still it stands serene.
What tides of peace, what surge of war
  That noble pine has seen!

For here before the white man's hour
  With hatchet, knife and bow
The Mohawk swept in savage power
  Against the Huron foe.

And here that sultry August day
  With shouldered pike and gun
Seth Warner led his rude array
  To fight at Bennington.

The land is fair, the kill runs clear,
  The mountains rise divine,
And peace and brotherhood are here
  Beneath the stately pine

That towers proudly toward the skies
  Unbent by many snows;
And "Freedom!" is the word it sighs
  On every wind that blows.

So may it brave the rudest blast,
  That time-defying tree,
A monument to all our past,
  A pledge of what shall be!

ℐ To a Cicada

Base insect, hush your strident, sizzling cry
    That doubles August heat! You gauze-winged pest,
Cicada, jarfly, locust, harvest fly,
    Why must you shrill and give the ear no rest?
But gentle Nature smiles and tells me why:
    "At first a maggot on the maple's bark,
This dropped to earth and burrowed deep to lie
    Among the roots and grow in nether dark
Springs, Summers, Autumns, Winters, seventeen
    Full years, till now emerging from the tomb
My minstrel comes, delightedly to preen
    His new-found wings, released from silent gloom
For three short weeks of warmth and love and light."
Sing on, small troubadour, you've earned the right!

¶ Bullied by Birds

The starlings have hatched in the nearest beech
A trio of nestlings, and bring to each
Twelve insects per hour. For Heaven's sake,
What horrible noises those starlets make!

Two swallows have built in our neat garage
A nest that is mud without camouflage;
Because of their little ones' appetites
We can't shut the door either days or nights.

A jay has appeared in his coat of blue;
He swears at our cat and the chipmunks, too,
And screams with that arrogant air of his,
"I'm boss of this ranch!"— and perhaps he is.

¶ Against Gardeners

Though calm, judicious gardening
Keeps arteries from hardening,
   The fad's too often carried to extremes;
So let's revile that vulture
And fiend of horticulture
   Who prosecutes his labors in his dreams.

While some believe in fairies,
In Ediths, Kates and Marys,
   Prospectuses and fluent demagogues,
This innocent reposes
His faith in growing roses
   As gorgeous as the plates in catalogues.

He shields his baby asters
And pinks from all disasters
   Immured within their kindergarten frames;
When seedlings give him trouble
And bend him almost double,
   He calls them by their horrid Latin names.

His only talk is babble
About his floral rabble,
   Delphiniums, calendulas and all;
His dahlias may look sickly,
But he'll revive them quickly,
   And they'll be simply wonderful in fall!

Then leave him, grubbing, seeding,
Transplanting, pruning, weeding,
   Correcting curvatures in hollyhocks,
Repelling aphids, weevils
And other crawly evils,
   A faithful shepherd, watering his phlox!

ℊ *Wild Orchard*

Woodchuck, rabbit, fawn,
This all again is yours, the men have gone;
From unkempt boughs, beside the tumbled wall,
Soft-thudding apples fall.

Chipmunk, squirrel, grouse,
Proud buck, mild doe and furtive whitefoot mouse,
Return, there is no longer aught to dread,
For you the feast is spread.

ℊ *First Snowfall*

Winnowed from Heaven it comes to bless
With beauty poor Earth's ugliness;
All that was foul is pure below
The absolution of the snow.

❡ Compliments of the Seasons

Our window-corner showed a happy sign,
   For there, uplifted for a place to cling,
We saw a tendriled wisp of budding vine
   And knew it for the calling-card of Spring.

Then in that self-same corner, spun with care
   To catch some reckless fly, some heedless hummer,
We saw the patient spider's filmy snare
   And knew that as the calling-card of Summer.

When Summer fled, when twilight hours were brief
   And early morning mists were over all,
The window-corner caught a drifting leaf,
   The gold-and-crimson calling-card of Fall.

We heard the blustery north wind's trumpet blow,
   We heard the tossing branches crack and splinter;
The corner held a triangle of snow,
   The ever-lovely calling-card of Winter.

¶ Short Cut

It's kinder to feet than the highway,
   And time can be saved, as a rule,
By taking that motorless byway,
   The well-trodden short cut to school.

Through marshes where osiers are bending,
   A grove with a fern-bordered pool,
And over a stile at the ending
   It leads you, the short cut to school.

Come follow it, wistfully turning
   From balsam woods fragrant and cool;
There's only one short cut to learning,
   The well-trodden short cut to school.

I awoke in silver moonlight long before your world
    was stirring,
For I heard the dogwood barking and the pussy-
    willow purring
And the faintest cowslip mooings from the fragrant
    meadow dairies,
So I knew that there were doings in the realm of
    Sprites and Fairies.

There were cricket chirps of clamor from the ferny
    forest border
Where the Hidden Folk were putting their affairs in
    proper order,
And they went in troops of twenties, or they worked
    in groups of sixes,
Getting food and making clothing for their youthful
    Pucks and Pixies.

First they gathered honeysuckle for those little
    nectar-sippers,
And they made them gloves of foxgloves, also shoes
    of lady-slippers;

They made them smocks of lady's-smocks with
    pokes of shepherd's-purses
In something less than half the time it takes to read
    these verses.

They made them caps of monkshoods with the
    daintiest of stitches,
And outing knickerbockers of the finest Dutchman's-
    breeches!

❡ Malt and Hops

Malt is a little Maltese,
　　Hops is a little black ace;
Malt is suspicious,
But Hops is ambitious
　　And frolics all over the place.

Malt will remain where you wish;
　　Hops, with his impudent phiz,
Skips, acrobatic,
From cellar to attic;
　　Nobody knows where he is.

Malt is a mannerly kit,
　　Hops never pauses nor stops.
What feline bratlings
Can equal our catlings,
　　Malt and tumultuous Hops!

❡ Sea Birds

Dear birds that love the wind and wave,
What lives are yours to lead, so brave
In gale or tempest, gallant, free
And glad — as life was meant to be!

❡ For All Young Things

Though little lambs are blithe to see
When gamboling on heath and hill,
The mournfullest of sights that be
Are little lambs when hurt or ill.

For all our little lambs a prayer
To which the world shall say, amen:
A kindly shepherd's healing care
Be theirs till they are whole again!

❡ *Epitaph on a Gallant Mare*

Strength, courage, beauty, where the comets play,
  Your four bright crescents overleap their bars
While on you gallop down the Milky Way
  To race with Pegasus among the stars.

❡ *The Desolater*

This is the forest's prime evil, the slovenly camper,
Wasting and spoiling and scattering litter and
　　rubbish,
Leaving his fire unquenched; what to him if its
　　embers
Kindle a blaze that shall sweep through the pines and
　　the birches
Miles upon miles in a fury of death and destruction!
This is the forest's prime evil, the reckless and
　　ruthless,
Let him be locked in a cell where a single barred
　　window
Looks on the flame-blackened ruins of beautiful
　　woodland!

¶ Storm

The brown brigades of Autumn leaves
    Assault the rampart of our hill;
A ruthless northwind drives and heaves
The brown brigades of Autumn leaves,
And though, bereft, the maple grieves
    Above her fallen children, still
The brown brigades of Autumn leaves
    Assault the rampart of our hill.

¶ Going and Staying

Two yellow warblers, a golden he and she,
A thrush and a phoebe are in our apple tree
Where all flute together, "The wind is blowing free,
    So we'll start for Carolina in the morning.
Away to Carolina and the swamps of Wateree,
To Georgia, Alabama, and the Matagorda Key;
Away to Nicaragua and the Caribbean Sea,
    Perhaps to Maracaibo in the morning!"

Gran'father Woodchuck, a patriarch is he,
And two lively chipmunks beneath our apple tree
Have frost-beaded whiskers and prudently agree
    To pack their Winter cellars in the morning.
"We'll pack our Winter cellars and as full as full
    can be,
For the days of dearth are coming and a hungry folk
    are we,
But we'll nibble, drowse, and listen to the merry
    chickadee
    When we've packed our Winter cellars in the
    morning!"

❡ Harvest Home

The maples flare among the spruces,
The bursting foxgrape spills its juices,
The gentians lift their sapphire fringes
On roadways rich with golden tinges,
The waddling woodchucks fill their hampers,
The deer mouse runs, the chipmunk scampers,
The squirrels scurry, never stopping,
For all they hear is apples dropping
And walnuts plumping fast and faster;
The bee weighs down the purple aster —
Yes, hive your honey, little hummer,
The woods are waving, "Farewell, Summer!"

⁊ Winterproof

The pipes are drained, the furnace flame has died,
 The rooms are all in order, every chair
Correctly covered; we have closed and tied
 The shutters that the windows shall not stare
Forlornly. So, we lock the door: Dear house,
 Good night, and may no storms that round you
 sweep,
No pert, intrusive chipmunk, nibbling mouse,
 Nor squirrel, scampering, disturb your sleep.
While earth is hard with frost and drifts enfold
 Your garden beds, but late so gay with flowers,
Rest well, belovèd home, and safely hold
 Our precious memories of happy hours
To greet us, like returning bluebirds, when
We light the fire upon your hearth again!